Crafts Canada

The useful arts

Una Abrahamson

Clarke, Irwin & Company Limited

Toronto   Vancouver

For Hilary and John

The author and publishers are indebted to the
following for supplying illustrative materials:

Peter Varley for photographs on pages 70,
102, 150,

Harold Whyte for photographs on pages 12, 28,

The Canadian Guild of Crafts (Ontario) for all the
photographs marked*, which are of works in their
Permanent Collection,

The Ontario Craft Foundation for photographs
of many works by Canadian craftsmen – and
to the craftsmen themselves, who granted us
permission to reproduce those photographs
in Crafts Canada,

The Canadian Guild of Crafts, Quebec,

The Royal Ontario Museum, the Nova Scotia
Museum, the Museum of the American Indian.

We are also grateful to those craftsmen who
supplied us with photographs of their own work
and that of their colleagues, or who made it
possible for us to have photographs taken.

Contents

Thanks & Acknowledgment

Wherever I went in my search for material for this book doors were opened. People gave generously of their time, and shared their experiences openly and warmly. I acknowledge with gratitude their courtesy and co-operation.

In particular I should like to thank: Dorothy Arnold, Toronto; Paul Bennett, Toronto; Bev de Jong, Calgary; Elizabeth Dingman, Toronto; Les Graff, Edmonton; The staff, Glenbow Foundation, Calgary; Viola Harris, Toronto; Mary Eileen Hogg, Toronto; Marjory Howard and staff, Sports & Recreation Bureau, Ontario; Helen Ignatieff, Toronto; John Ikeda, Lethbridge; Alice M. S. Lighthall, Montreal; Luke Lindoe, Medicine Hat; Alex MacDonald, Toronto; Olga Manastyzsky, Edmonton; Adelaide Marriott, Toronto; Douglas Motter and Associates, Calgary; Carol Mullinger, Calgary; Irene Pawlykowsky, Edmonton; J. Stan Perrot, Calgary, and the staff of the Alberta College of Art; John Porter, Medicine Hat; Doris Ramsay, Calgary; Mary Skrypnyk, Toronto; Jos Storm, Banff; Eileen Taylor, Calgary; Guy Vidal, St. Adele en Haut; Carol Watkinson, Lethbridge; Robert W. Whyte, Edmonton; Betty Ann Yuill, Medicine Hat.

It is conventional to thank wives and typists. I have none, but I do thank my children, Hilary and John, who often made my meals and bed when I was immersed in the manuscript.

I am indebted to Joan Chalmers of the World Craft Council and Alan Campaigne of the Canadian Guild of Crafts, who suggested it was time to write about Canadian crafts and who first enthused me. And I thank Larry S. Loomer of Windsor, Nova Scotia for his constant encouragement, and Scott Robson of the Halifax Museum who shared his knowledge of pioneer crafts with me. Michael Wilcox of Woodview, Ontario and Joyce Chown of Sheridan College, Mississauga were also extremely helpful.

I wish also to express my appreciation to Hugh Michaelson who designed this book and made it beautiful so that it records Canadian crafts suitably; to Ruth DonCarlos, my editor, who became my friend; and to Marguerite McLean who remains my friend after organizing the research.

And last of all, I wish to thank the Canada Council whose grant made travel possible and life smoother.

The omissions are my own.

Preface

In the two years I have been writing this book, I have travelled far and learned much. Like many people with a range of interests that includes Canadiana in all its aspects, from books and printing to treen, furniture and textiles, I thought I knew a great deal about crafts and craftsmen. But crafts have changed radically of recent years; some have disappeared, some have been revived, and others have made their appearance for the first time. Meeting the people currently working in the field and listening to their struggles has humbled me, and at the same time has given me an understanding of contemporary crafts that I hope others will share with me.

It has been an uphill fight to breathe new life into Canadian crafts which for many years stagnated or struggled to survive. There was a widespread belief that articles made by machine were superior to articles made by hand. There was a pervasive feeling that anything brought in from abroad was better than a similar product made at home. And there was a welter of poorly designed and badly-made craft objects which crowded the worthwhile pieces off the stage for many years. Nevertheless, as I discovered in the course of my research, a renaissance has taken place in the last twenty years and there is an enthusiasm and excitement among the workers which is catching.

Not all is perfect by any means, but considering the general atmosphere of indifference that prevailed for so long, amazing progress has been made. In some disciplines Canadian craftsmen can compete with others working in any part of the world. And this, I hope, will provide added stimulus which will be further enhanced by the establishment of craft museums in various parts of the country.

Una Abrahamson
Toronto, February, 1974

The photographs on pages 16, 17, 20, 24, 25, 33, 54, 75, 82, 84, 115, 146, 159, 163 were selected as entries in the 1974 World Crafts Exhibition.

Introduction

What is the difference between art and craft? It has been suggested that art is activity that begins with the head, whereas craft is activity that begins with the hands. Some people feel, however, that the difference lies in the intention of the creator. They contend that the basic purpose of art is to provide enjoyment, whereas the basic purpose of craft is to produce something useful.

The fact of the matter is that there is often very little distinction between a work of art and a work of craftsmanship. And the two disciplines are growing closer together all the time. In pioneer days it was taken for granted that a weaver would produce a fabric that might very well be handsome but would most certainly be useful. Today he is more apt to produce a decorative piece that will delight the eye but serve no practical function at all.

The change is largely due to the rise of manufacture. Several generations ago it was believed that the machine would drive the craftsman out of existence. It almost did. But the winds of change have brought about a new craft climate. The designer-craftsman, no longer obliged to turn out necessities, is now free to give his attention to work that may or may not be useful, but that is, above all, a unique expression of his own creative talents. In craft after craft the same pattern emerges: the artisan has become an artist.

Not all people who work with their hands, of course, can be justly termed designer-craftsmen. Many are content to follow the patterns established by others, adapting colours and details to suit their own particular taste. They find a great recreational value in the pursuit of handicraft hobbies which provide relief from the pressure of modern living.

This aspect of the occupation has undoubtedly contributed to the recent widespread upsurge in craft practice. But it is only one aspect of a many-faceted phenomenon. The need for outlets which will permit people to preserve their individuality in a faceless, mass-production society is even more important. And it is this drive which has caused many people to engage in crafts not as hobbies but as serious – often full-time – pursuits. They are the workers who are setting the pace in international crafts today, who are moving away from traditional designs and techniques to explore new methods and new ideas.

This does not mean that the traditional crafts have died out, however. Concurrent with the rise of new approaches there has been a revival of interest in old techniques. Crafts known to former generations now flourish side by side with new ones. For example, bookbinding, glass-blowing and paper-making, once almost forgotten arts, are today enjoying a renaissance. This trend is particularly evident in Canada, where the pioneer crafts are receiving a great deal of attention at the present time.

In identifying with pioneer craftsmen, Canadian workers are perpetuating a solid tradition. For many years after the first settlers were brought over from France crafts played an important part in the social and cultural life of this country. Schools for artisans were established in New France at an early date, and the convents stressed the importance of fine needlework. This resulted in a high level of workmanship which the Quebec government has nurtured. In the Atlantic provinces the impact of world trade in the heyday of the sailing ships created a demand for sophisticated wares which spurred the local craftsmen to greater achievements. In Canada generally the United Empire Loyalists, many of whom had come from affluent homes in settled communities, produced articles that showed remarkable ingenuity, and their desire for professionally-made household furnishings attracted trained workers. As the west opened up, the immigrants who flooded in from Europe brought a new wave of folk arts, many of which have continued to thrive in ethnic communities across the country.

Inevitably the crafts in Canada declined as the factory system took hold. It was not until the *Art Nouveau* movement brought about a revival of interest, that encouraging things began to happen on the European and Canadian craft scenes.

All during those dark ages, however, there were individuals and groups who strove to keep the crafts alive. The women were particularly active in organizing exhibitions, arranging for competitions to be judged on the basis of international standards, and in founding and supporting organizations to foster arts and crafts.

At the beginning of the twentieth century a number of Montreal women, working with the Women's Art Association, began a campaign to conserve and revive crafts, and in 1902 the group, which later became the Canadian Handicrafts Guild and eventually the Canadian Guild of Crafts, opened a shop in Montreal. Ever since, the group has collected, exhibited and sold hand-crafted articles from all over Canada. The Guild was also instrumental in setting up craft centres in Labrador in response to an appeal from Dr. Wilfred Grenfell of the Grenfell Misson, and it has performed yeoman service by acting as a central advisory body for similar movements everywhere in Canada.

Much was also done by The Outport Nursing Committee in Newfoundland. Originally organized in 1920 to provide nursing and medical care for people living in isolated settlements, the committee worked out a scheme whereby women could earn money to assist with the expenses of the services by knitting and weaving in their own homes. The name of the group was then changed to Newfoundland Outport Nurses' Industrial Association, NONIA became the trade name of the work produced, and the nurses were known as Nonia nurses. Wool and instructions are sent to local committees by a central organization which also handles sales.

It is fortunate that the women were concerned and that dedicated craftsmen continued to work, for it took forty years for the Royal Canadian Academy to become aware that interesting craft-work was being done in Canada. Their 1943 exhibition was the first at which they permitted a showing of "handicrafts."

Canadian crafts in general have benefitted from the world-wide interest in hand-work. The immigrants who have come to this country since World War II have brought with them their rich heritage of craft techniques and have stimulated a curiosity about present trends in other parts of the world. The standards established by the great international craft schools are increasingly important to Canadian craftsmen and collectors, and there is a constant upgrading of design and workmanship. This has been fostered by the World Craft Council, the Canadian Guild of Crafts and provincial and local organizations. The emphasis on craft courses in schools of practical arts reflects the current concern for the preservation of traditional skills and does much to encourage the development of innovative techniques.

11

Ceramics

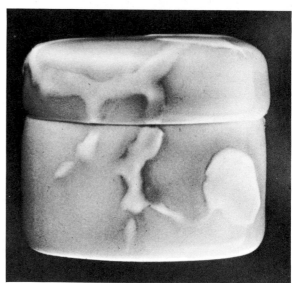

*Pot by Roman Bartkiw, Markdale, Ontario**

*Weed bottle by Marion Lewis, Toronto, Ontario**

*Porcelain bottle by Bailey Leslie, Toronto, Ontario**

*Translucent porcelain box by Enid Sharon LeGros, Paspébiac, Quebec**

Clay, the basis of all ceramics, has been worked for over six thousand years, and is still being worked today very much as it was in the beginning.

There have been milestones in the potter's craft, of course. The first development was the discovery that fire would harden a clay object more efficiently than the sun. The second was that a pot baked in an enclosed oven was sturdier than a pot simply placed beside or in a fire. Other changes have included the invention of the potter's wheel (about three thousand years ago in Egypt), the development of improved glazes, made possible by a more exact knowledge of mineralogy and chemistry, and the invention of the thermostatically-controlled kiln. But in essence the process remains the same as when man first shaped a rude clay vessel.

There are three basic types of ceramics – earthenware, stoneware and porcelain. The difference between them lies in the raw materials employed and in the temperatures at which they are fired.

In the raw state clays are filled with tiny mineral particles which determine their colour, texture and malleability. Earthenware is made of clay which may be red, brown, gray or yellow. Stoneware is made of clay with a high iron content, and porcelain is made of a finely textured white clay mixture.

Earthenware, which is fired at a relatively low temperature, is porous, and must be glazed and refired before it will hold liquid. Stoneware, fired at a higher temperature, does not need glazing, although if common salt is thrown into the kiln it vaporizes and forms a transparent glaze that enhances the finished product. Porcelain, which is fired at a very high temperature (above 2600°F.), is hard, non-absorbent and semi-translucent.

Prior to 500 B.C. all pottery was earthenware. Then the Chinese began to fire their pots at a higher temperature, and during the Han period, 202 B.C. to 220 A.D., their potters succeeded in making objects that were impervious to liquids without glazing. They had, in effect, perfected the art of making stoneware. Eventually, centuries before the Western potters, they also discovered the secret of making porcelain. It is therefore quite appropriate that dishes in general and porcelain in particular came to be known by the name of the country in which the major developments took place.

Wherever pottery is made, however, the first step is the preparation of the material. Stones and unwanted impurities are eliminated and the clay is kneaded to remove air bubbles. Once that is done, the craftsman is free to choose several methods of forming the

*Stoneware tea set by Ruth Gowdy McKinley, Mississauga, Ontario**

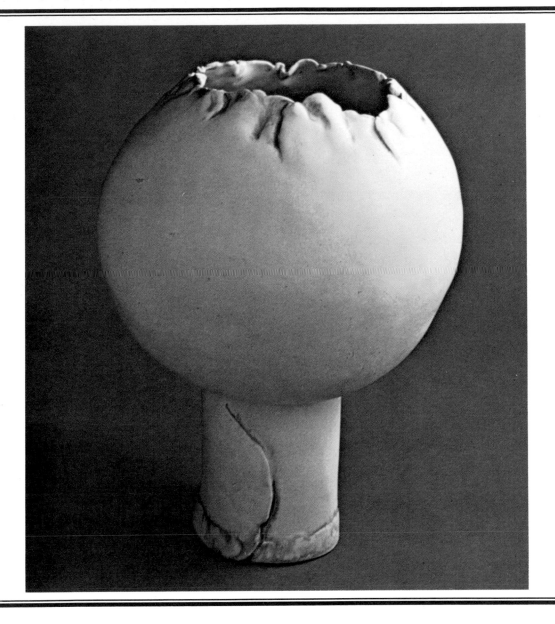

*Porcelain wine server by Ruth Gowdy McKinley, Mississauga, Ontario**

object. He may select the slab method, in which a lump of clay is rolled to an even thickness, then manipulated by hands or tools into shape. Or he may select the ancient coil technique, in which clay is formed into long rolls, then circled round and round to the shape and size required. The coils can be left in that state or the surface can be smoothed.

It is believed that it was from the coil technique that the potter's wheel developed. The wheel is basically a horizontal plate centred on a vertical drive shaft which is twirled to spin the plate. A ball of clay is thrown on to the plate and as the shaft turns the potter forces both thumbs into the clay. At the same time his hands draw up, and he guides the sides of the pot to counteract the centrifugal force which throws them outwards.

When a potter wants to repeat shapes or make standardized objects such as tiles, bowls or plates, he generally uses a mould. The simplest method of moulding is to press a slab of clay over or into a mould. As soon as the clay is dry, the shaped slab is lifted off and left to dry further in the air.

Slip casting is more complicated. In this case the mould consists of two plaster halves with a cavity between. The liquid clay is poured into the cavity and when it has hardened sufficiently to hold its shape, the mould is removed.

Sand casting is also used for repeated shapes. For this, a shape – usually one half of a symmetrical object – is moulded out of wet sand. Then plaster is poured over the mould and left to harden. Finally, a clay slab is laid on the inside of the plaster shell, where it remains until it is dry enough to hold its shape. It is then removed and the process is repeated. The two halves are joined together by scoring the sides and cementing them with "slip," a mixture of clay and water.

After the pot has been coiled, turned, or moulded, it is allowed to air dry. When the excess moisture has evaporated, the pieces are fired, then glazed and fired again at a higher temperature, to mature the clay and melt the glaze.

The glazing operation has changed very little since it was first developed by the ancient Egyptians, and the colours and finishes achieved during the great classical Chinese and Greek periods have never been surpassed. Basically, the process consists of painting the surface of a pot with a solution which is then fused by heat to form a glass-like coating.

The application, mixing and firing of glazes is complicated, and the colour depends on a variety of factors: the composition of the glaze, the degree of heat, the position of the object in the kiln, and even the amount of oxygen in the kiln. So it is easy to understand

why so many potters guard their secrets jealously. Even today, when a great deal is known about heat, minerals and chemical action, and when kilns are thermostatically controlled, there are still surprised potters.

Wherever clay is found, pottery of one kind or another has been made. On the North American continent the Eskimos worked in clay as long ago as the ninth century. On warm sunny days they made earthenware from a clay mixture thickened with sand and bird's feathers.

Some Eskimos shaped their vessels by shoving one hand inside the lump while beating the exterior with the other hand or with a stick. Others made their pots by cementing clay walls to a stone base with a mixture of clay and seal blood strengthened by male dog hair. (It was believed that the hairs of bitches would prevent cementing.) Designs were applied by corrugating, impressing, and incising the wet clay. The pots were then set before a small fire, and were turned frequently so that they would dry evenly.

This earthenware was very brittle and it disintegrated in wet weather. In an attempt to strengthen it, Western Arctic Eskimos coated the exterior with seal or reindeer blood, and when that had dried they filled the pot with oil and left it there until penetration had made the clay less brittle.

Eskimos are still making ceramics from local clay, but now the ancient skills have been forgotten, and the contemporary Eskimo potter follows modern techniques taught by teachers from the south. He no longer makes household pots, but turns out figures and bowls. His designs, however, are unusual. At the same time primitive and sophisticated, they have been compared to the work of the Etruscans and the Aztecs.

The North American Indians too made earthenware wherever clay was obtainable, and since they did not have the potter's wheel, they used the coiling and modelling techniques. They knew how to glaze and were efficient craftsmen.

Indian pottery reflected the tastes and talents of the tribe; each group had its own distinctive style. Traditional designs were so firmly entrenched, in fact, that there was little scope for inventiveness.

Today, like the Eskimos, Indians are once again making pottery. Some of them are producing very contemporary pieces which bear little relationship to their ancient designs. Others are employing traditional patterns, but are giving them a modern application.

Slip casting is used for making a number of identical items. It consists of pouring "slip" (clay in liquid suspension) into a mould, as shown, allowing it to harden, and then removing the formed piece, which is subsequently glazed and fired. The moulds may be bought from suppliers or may be made by the potter himself, from a master piece. Though most craftsmen now prefer to make individual, distinctive pieces, many find that the painting and decorating of the "mass-produced" items allows them sufficient scope for their creative talents and permits them to turn out sets of dishes in their own design.

Footed pot by Bailey Leslie, Toronto, Ontario

Ceramics by Zeljko Kujndzic, Kelowna, British Columbia

Porcelain bottle by Ruth Gowdy McKinley, Mississauga, Ontario*

Porcelain vase by Raimondo Cittadini, Windsor, Ontario*

Stoneware vase by John Hamilton Shaw, Fredericton, New Brunswick*

Bottle by Tess Kidick, Jordan, Ontario*

Floor jar by Joan Bobbs, Markham, Ontario*

Porcelain vase by Norine Rive, Willowdale, Ontario*

The settlers in New France also made pottery, though to a limited extent since the colony was discouraged from establishing its own industries. It was only when the supply ships failed to arrive that the habitants made their own pots and crockery, following the methods and patterns learned in their homeland.

Later a few potteries were set up in the Maritimes, and they produced earthenware that closely resembled its English counterpart. These establishments were short-lived, however, because they could not compete with the imports from Great Britain. Upper Canada fared better; it eventually had more potteries than all the rest of the country combined. But that didn't amount to more than two dozen factories, and they survived only because they had the good luck to be away from the seaports. The fact of the matter was that Canadian potteries in the nineteenth century could not prosper because of the massive importing of ceramics from Britain and the United States. Even protective tariffs could not prevent the foreign domination of the industry.

Pottery-making remained a strong cottage industry, however. A few enterprising families produced earthenware from local clay, and marketed it within a radius of about twenty miles. The result of this was that regional designs were developed and ethnic traditions were kept alive.

Both methods of pottery production were carried on for the greater part of the nineteenth century. Simple table wares were made in the homes, with few mechanical aids. Most such items were earthenware and required glazing. The materials for that operation were difficult to come by, however. The principal component, lead, had to be salvaged from the liners of tea cases, and the other main ingredient, copper, had to be rescued from scrap. The heavy work of grinding the metal to a fine powder that could be mixed with the other glaze ingredients was done by the entire family, including the children, as part of the household chores.

More complicated ceramic pieces such as pitchers and teapots were generally turned out by the factories and were moulded in a press.

Most factories specialized in either stoneware or earthenware. Stoneware potteries were always located close to rivers so that the raw materials could be transported directly to the factory by water. Clay of the quality required for stoneware had to be imported from New Jersey, since most indigenous clays sagged under the high kiln heat. The potters, too, generally came from the United States, as they were familiar with the working of that type

Compote by Bailey Leslie, Toronto, Ontario*

Stoneware table with glass top by Mary Keepax, Ballinafad, Ontario*

of material. Consequently, most Canadian stoneware shows an American influence.

In general, Canadian pottery was severely practical, but many potters were sufficiently skilled to satisfy the customers who demanded ornamental ware. Glazed earthenware spaniels were frequently purchased for mantlepieces, and pots to hold the jungle of houseplants so beloved of the Victorians were much in demand. Earthenware picture frames, tobacco jars, and charming money boxes that were supposed to encourage thrift in small children were also produced.

Eventually, the competition from abroad proved too much for both the commercial and cottage industries. The imported pottery was so much finer than the home-made product that the demand for the latter gradually dwindled away, and by the beginning of the twentieth century had practically disappeared. The factories too were soon outclassed by the larger foreign plants that had more up-to-date equipment, and one by one they went out of business.

In the late nineteenth century a passion for hand-painted china swept over the Western world, and most of the middle-class women of Canada were caught up in it. This was partly due to the fact that finely-decorated imported china was very expensive at the time, and partly to the fact that china painting was a pleasant, rewarding occupation for people with artistic leanings. In any case the fad caught on. China was painted in cities and in villages all across the country. Courses were offered from Halifax to Saskatoon. Blanks of porcelain plates, cups and comports were imported in great quantity from the finest manufacturers in Europe and Japan. Then suddenly, with the coming of the First World War, the whole phenomenon came to an abrupt end. The china blanks could no longer be imported, and all at once there were other, more serious matters to be attended to. Many hand-painted pieces of china are still in existence, however – cherished reminders of another era. And of those quite a few are excellent examples of good design and skilled craftsmanship.

Today there is a renaissance in the hand-crafting of ceramics, and some interesting pieces of earthenware, stoneware and porcelain are being produced in Canada.

This is not the first time that such a revival has taken place. Around 1880 craftsmen, in protest against the harmful influence of mass production, returned to hand potting. They rejected moulds and presses and retained only the potter's wheel. And they turned to

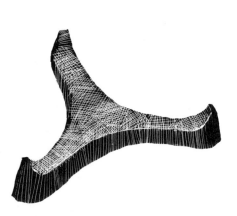

classical ceramics for their inspiration. Out of this movement grew craft societies and potters' guilds that restored the old standards of workmanship.

Early in the twentieth century the revival was given impetus by the students of the Bauhaus school who became interested in the work of a few folk potters who continued to use the methods of a bygone era. The young designers adopted their techniques and produced simple, functional pottery that started a general trend toward simplicity.

In the 1940's the reassessment was stimulated by the work of a number of European trained potters, including Kjeld and Erica Deichmann of New Brunswick and Sibyl Laubental of Alberta. It was the simple yet supremely sophisticated objects produced in their workshops that made the Canadian public aware of, and receptive to, contemporary hand-made pottery.

Today potters are influenced not only by the classicists and the function-oriented designers, however. They are interested in everything from Indian and Eskimo totemic figures to Japanese symbolism. A growing number of them are experimenting with Raku, a free-form pottery that is ancient in concept.

Raku was introduced to Japan by Korean potters at the time of Genghis Khan and became the traditional ceramic for the ceremonial tea bowls. It is a very exacting discipline and to be successful at it the potter must have a high standard of taste. Because the results are variable, a great deal of discarding is necessary.

In making raku the free-form clay object is glazed immediately after it is formed, and then is fired in a kiln until the lead-based glaze has fused. Immediately that stage has been reached, the pieces are removed from the kiln and during the short time the glaze is moulten the potter modifies the object, changing the patterns or swirling the liquid glaze around. The cooled pot is then plunged into cold water.

The raku process in the West differs considerably from the Eastern practice. It is free of the codified rules set down by the Japanese and includes several steps they do not take: the modification of the moulten glaze, for example.

Because industry is now manufacturing handsome, functional ware at economical prices, the craft potter is released from the necessity to produce repetitive pieces. He is free to choose his own direction and to make each item unique. Though some craftsmen are involved in semi-production, turning out sets of bowls, cups and utensils, others are creating objects which range from homely casseroles to giant murals.

27

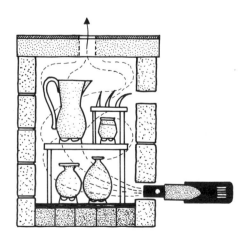

Firing the clay is a delicate operation. The kiln must be loaded so that the pieces do not touch, and the pots should be placed on three-cornered stands, or stilts, so that the hot air will circulate freely. The temperature must be raised gradually and uniformly. And when the firing is complete (as determined by observing, through a peephole, cones of clay which serve as indicators), the kiln must be allowed to cool slowly. The process takes eight hours or more.

Glass

Glass is a remarkable substance. It is sometimes unbreakable, sometimes extremely brittle. It is sometimes transparent, sometimes opaque. It both reflects and absorbs light. It has been known for centuries, yet its properties are still not fully explored.

Man probably first encountered glass in one of its natural forms. Since the basic ingredients for the substance are silica sand, an alkali (usually potash or soda), and lime, all fused at a very high temperature, it is not surprising that glass sometimes occurs as a result of a physical phenomenon. When lightning strikes sand the heat may melt it to produce slender glass tubes known as petrified lightning. Similarly, the heat of a volcanic eruption sometimes causes rocks and sand to coalesce into a form of glass called obsidian, which was used by primitive man to make knives, arrowheads and jewellery.

Once he had managed to imitate nature and produce glass by his own efforts, man probably had very little difficulty in forming it into simple shapes. A hole dug in sand or earth serves as a mould, and the molten glass poured into it soon hardens into a solid object, or even a bowl-shaped vessel.

The making of hollow vessels, however, is a more sophisticated process. In early times a core of sand held by a metal rod was repeatedly dipped into molten glass, rolled and smoothed, so that a thick layer of glaze-like glass adhered to the core. The core was removed after the glass had cooled.

In the first century A.D., it was discovered that red-hot soft glass could be blown into a bubble, and that it could be coaxed into a multitude of shapes. Since then the glass-blower's pipe has been the most important instrument involved in the production of craft glass. Modern glass-making techniques include blowing, moulding, and even the primitive sand-casting method.

Although the secret of making glass was discovered in the Near East, the art is essentially a Western one. The process was developed by European craftsmen after the first century A.D., possibly with the assistance of migrant Jewish workers, and it has remained predominantly a Western craft ever since.

The oldest glass objects known were found in Egypt and Babylon, and date from the third millenium B.C. The Egyptians used precious stones and glass side by side, apparently valuing them equally. The burial treasure of Tutankhamen, now in the Cairo Museum, includes gold surfaces inlaid with lapis-lazuli, turquoise – and jasper-red glass.

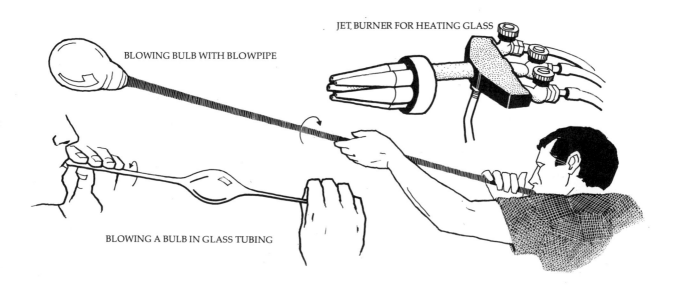

JET BURNER FOR HEATING GLASS

BLOWING BULB WITH BLOWPIPE

BLOWING A BULB IN GLASS TUBING

The art of glass-making received little impetus in ancient Greece, probably because the art of pottery was so highly developed that there was no demand for household glass. But glass objects were part of the booty prized by Persian and Egyptian armies and were valuable enough to be carried in triumphal processions. The Romans also prized glass, and prior to the fall of the Empire there were extensive private collections of it.

The collapse of the Roman Empire affected glass manufacturing, because it ended the trade from Egypt to the Rhine (then the centre of European glass-making), cutting off the supply of soda, which was used in the production process. But in the seventh century a substitute for soda was discovered by the northern glass-makers. It was found that potash, readily obtainable from beechwood ashes, produced a glass which was both sturdier and heavier than the ancient soda-glass.

Venice continued to make soda-glass, however, because her trading connections with Egypt still held. Venetian glass has ever since differed from that of the rest of Europe, especially as Venice, during the Renaissance, developed a unique pattern of culture which was reflected in the designs of the thin-walled glass made there. Unfortunately, today Venetian glass has become so commercialized that it has lost some of its original freshness of concept.

New trends in glass design began to be apparent in the sixteenth century, particularly in the Rhineland where experiments with painted glass were underway. This was not an original concept. Enamel painting had reached a high standard in Syria and Persia in the thirteenth and fourteenth centuries, and the technique had worked its way north by way of Venice where it had been in vogue in the early fifteenth century. But the Germans adapted the enamelling technique to glass.

Another important innovation was the introduction of cut glass. At the end of the sixteenth century, Caspar Lehmann of Prague first applied the cutting and engraving techniques used on rock crystal to glass. And in the late seventeenth century the Bohemians discovered that the addition of potash-lime made it possible to produce a glass so thick that it could be engraved in high relief. Subsequently, in the eighteenth century, English glass-makers found that if lead was used as an additive the glass took on a diamond-like quality. At the same time their cutting techniques became very sophisticated.

The first glass house, or factory, in North America is believed to have been located at Jamestown, Virginia, a colony founded in 1607 by Captain John Smith who was financed

SQUEEZING NECK OF BOTTLE

Glass blowing is an ancient method of shaping glass. It involves heating the glass to a molten state and then blowing air into it through a pipe to form a bubble which can be shaped in various ways while it is hot. For example, it can be turned into a vase by pressing it against a flat surface to make a base and squeezing it with tongs to form a neck. While he is blowing, the craftsman twirls the pipe to counteract the pull of gravity.

by the London Company. The second group of settlers to land at Jamestown included eight Dutch and Polish glass-makers, and there is evidence that a serious attempt was made to manufacture glass there.

The craft of glass-making did not spread to Canada for almost two hundred years. It seems unlikely that glass was produced under the French regime, since the authorities in France did not encourage colonial enterprise. Certainly no shards or other evidence have as yet been found to indicate that there was such an industry. The British conquerors adhered to these same economic policies; in fact, in 1763, George III issued an edict discouraging any new manufacturing in Canada.

It was left to an enterprising United Empire Loyalist, Nathaniel Mallory, to establish the first glass factory in Canada. He settled at Mallorytown, Leeds County, Ontario in 1784, and soon became a successful entrepreneur. He had a cordwood business, a pack train that brought supplies from Montreal and Kingston, a brickyard, and other interests. It is believed that he established his glass house about 1825 and that it survived until the winter of 1839-40, when it disappeared owing to a labour dispute.

By that time, however, the glass industry was taking root in Canada, and though the market was small and competition from the United States was strong, it continued to grow. By the end of the nineteenth century there were leading glass houses at Trenton in Nova Scotia, Vaudreuil in Quebec, and Napanee and Hamilton in Ontario.

Glass blowers were the aristocracy of Canadian labour. Their pay was high, but they earned it, working under almost insufferable conditions in temperatures over 100°F. (In the summer months most glass houses were forced to stop work entirely.) Once a year the blowers celebrated by marching in Labour Day parades wearing glass hats and carrying glass swords, knives, pistols and canes.

For the most part, early Canadian glass was mass produced and utilitarian, but the blowers satisfied their desire for craftsmanship by producing some free-blown pieces, the most important of which were whimseys. The term "whimsey" is used to designate an unusual piece of glass made by a blower to show his versatility and control of the medium. Such pieces were never sold, but were made as gifts. Hammers, canes, paperweights and swords were the most common whimseys, but glass drapes, an unusual and uniquely Canadian type of ornament, were also made. The drapes (really swags made of glass chains) were used to decorate walls and mantels, and were much sought after by

Glass decanter by Robert D. Held, Mississauga, Ontario*

innkeepers, who paid for them in kind – by providing the glass blowers with beer. They were very perishable, however, and few are in existence today.

The nineteenth-century *Art Nouveau* movement had an important effect on the glass industry. The French artist, Emile Gallé, and the American, L. C. Tiffany, who took Far Eastern glass as their inspiration, were particularly influential. Much of the Gallé glass resembles porcelain, and when held against the light, has the appearance of Chinese jade. The Tiffany pieces have coppery metallic surfaces.

It was the introduction of such innovative practices that paved the way for the transformations of the twentieth century. Certainly the changes in glass-making techniques in this century have been revolutionary. The developments include glass that is iron hard, glass that is elastic, and glass that can be spun into threads and turned into fabric.

The astounding inventiveness and competence of twentieth-century Scandinavian glass-makers has been particularly important. This is all the more surprising because Swedish glass was an off-shoot of German manufacturing, and there was no long and indigenous tradition of glass-making in that country. Perhaps it is for this very reason – because they were not hampered by tradition – that the designers and craftsmen of Sweden and Finland have produced some of the most distinguished work of this century and have had a profound effect on public taste.

There have been two principal trends in twentieth-century glass. The 1930's brought an appreciation of thick, undecorated objects and austere, massive forms. Under the influence of the Bauhaus school, function became the all-important factor. Spherical or tear-shaped pieces became popular, and glass once again relied on its own natural appearance for beauty, without distracting decoration.

In the 1950's, craftsmen's eyes tired of the ultra simple, which by then had lost its freshness. They turned to nuances of colour and contrasts of texture. The idea of function and emphasis on the nature of glass were still important, but a new freedom in form appeared. The craft returned to its beginnings and a new search to express its beauty began.

This search has been apparent in North America since the end of World War II, when courses in glass-making were introduced into art schools. In 1959, the American Crafts Council Conference at Lake George, New York, discussed glass, particularly blown glass,

To cut glass the worker holds the article against a revolving wheel of sandstone or carborundum, and guides it so that the wheel wears away the glass along the pattern lines previously marked out.

Stained glass bird by Ellen Simon, New York, New York

Off-hand blown glass vase by Michael Robinson, Chatham, Ontario

Glass bottle by Michael Robinson, Chatham, Ontario*

Fumed glass vase by Ellen Issenman, Toronto, Ontario

Glass bottle by Robert D. Held, Mississauga, Ontario

as an artist's medium and a craft discipline. The distinction was made between the maker of "art glass" – expensive decorative objects such as bowls, animals and sculpture – and the artist glass-maker who turns to glass as a medium of self-expression, frequently after study in other fields. The numbers of these craftsmen are growing constantly and new developments are constantly taking place in this field.

Today Canadian glass-makers, like those in other parts of the world, are once again exploring the potentialities of the medium. There is now greater emphasis on free-form and much less on traditional shapes. The personal taste and satisfaction of the craftsman is an important factor, and there is a continual search for the unusual. Vibrant colours are widely used for special effects, and all manner of materials – wire, beads, cereal grains – are employed to create patterns and textures.

Stained Glass

After several hundred years of decline, the ancient craft of stained glass is now being revived and rethought. Craftsmen are breaking out of the narrow confines of sentimental religious decoration and turning to the use of colour for its own sake, as a medium for the creation of works of art that arouse in the beholder a sense of wonder.

The use of stained glass as window decoration dates back to ancient times when Moslem designers fitted small pieces of coloured glass into intricate window traceries of stone, wood or plaster to produce superb abstract mosaics. In the West it was used in church windows as early as the fifth century, and by the tenth century pictorial windows were being made. Ever since, stained glass has been primarily used for church decoration, and the craftsmen working in this field to this day employ Christian symbols which were once understood by all. Many colours have their own special meaning, and there are emblems to represent the Godhead, the apostles, the saints and the orders of cherubim. Since the artists incorporate these symbols in their designs, a true appreciation of the windows requires an understanding of religious images.

It is believed that the first stained-glass windows were made by monks who used a red-hot iron to cut the coloured glass. The pieces were then fitted into channelled lead strips and soldered together at junction points. (The leads were adjusted to the design and formed an integral part of it.)

The glass was coloured by immersing it in a melting pot where metallic oxides fused with it. Considering the comparative crudity of the method, remarkable colour variations were achieved. Moreover, the uneven surface and varying thickness of the early glass served to heighten the scintillating effect of the light refraction.

Only fragments of the earliest stained-glass windows remain, but we know that they were characterized by dark rich colours, and that the designs incorporated single figures and decorative scrollwork. Gradually the designs became more detailed and the range of colours broader. Various shades of red, blue, green and purple were used, in conjunction with small amounts of white glass. As time went on, the white areas became increasingly important for the depiction of heavenly hosts, and by the fifteenth century some of this glass had a metallic finish which produced a silvery glow.

By the sixteenth century the task of the stained-glass worker was simplified by the fact that glass was available in larger, smoother pieces. And towards the middle of that century the development of special enamel paints made it possible to paint designs on glass and then fire it. As a result there was an emphasis on large-scale realism.

And then the craft began to decline. Not only were many of the fine stained-glass windows destroyed during the Reformation, Civil Wars and Puritan revolutions, but there was a change in taste and a deterioration in craftsmanship. It has been suggested that the decline in aesthetic taste set in when secular rather than spiritual values became predominant in society. Whatever the reason, there was a decided shift in techniques and approach.

During the eighteenth century, the change in style was particularly marked. The characteristic boldness was rejected in favour of mellow compositions which aped academic painting. The only concession to religion was in the subject matter, and even this deteriorated. The figures portrayed became stereotyped, archly-sentimental representations of patron saints, and personifications such as Peace, Faith and Hope.

To achieve an oil-painting effect, the traditional practice of leading in small pieces of pre-coloured glass was abandoned. Instead larger and larger panes of transparent glass, coloured with paint and enamel, were incorporated. The only connection the new method had with the old was that the same materials – glass, lead and pigments – were used.

It is a moot point whether the Gothic Revival in architecture helped or hindered the stained-glass business. It provided work for artisans, but gave no encouragement to

Stained glass panel by Stephen Taylor, Toronto, Ontario

original contemporary design, and the repetition of traditional designs by those who continued to practise the ancient technique brought about a new low in the craft.

By the beginning of the nineteenth century the few traditionalists who continued to work generally executed nothing but heraldic designs, and eventually even this activity petered out. The fancy fanlights and decorated windows so popular for domestic establishments were mainly merely coloured glass. True stained-glass windows were seldom produced, even for churches, and those that were made were generally devoid of freshness, charm and piety.

There were exceptions to this rule, of course. The Swiss, in particular, produced some charming and colourful domestic stained glass during this period. But the overall output was pretty dismal.

In the late nineteenth century a movement began to revive the art of making true stained glass. The drive was largely initiated by the artist-poet William Morris, who advocated a return to the ideals of the mediaeval world. And it was supported by others with similar views, including the artist Burne-Jones. But though a number of craftsmen were caught up in this revival, they frequently lacked vision, boldness — even know-how — and continued to turn out timid period pieces. As a result, the advancement of contemporary design was painfully slow. Perhaps that is why the craft was restricted to church decoration for so many years.

In recent years the revival has gained new impetus, however, stimulated by commissions given to painters in the mainstream of contemporary art. John Piper, Fernand Leger, Marc Chagall, Georges Rouault and Henri Matisse have all made important contributions to the craft. The fact that they have been able to do so is evidence that modern techniques in painting and design can be directly translated into glass without transgressing the fundamentals of either art form. Like contemporary tapestry, stained glass, whether religious or secular, offers a challenge to the creative artist.

Canada has a tradition of producing high quality stained glass, and over the years has been fortunate enough to have a number of excellent designer-craftsmen working in this field.

One of the most interesting and prolific of the producers was the Canada Stained Glass Works, founded by Joseph McCausland who advertised in the 1850's that he was a

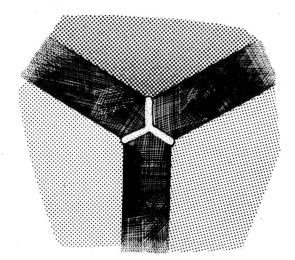

The making of stained glass is a painstaking operation. The pieces of coloured glass are cut according to a working drawing, are painted with enamels and fired, and are put together with channeled strips of lead which are soldered at the junction points as shown.

Pierced stained glass screen by Stephen Taylor, Toronto, Ontario

painter, decorator and enameller on glass. In the 1880's the company was joined by McCausland's son Robert, who had studied in England and who was elected an associate designer member of the Royal College of Art at the age of twenty-five. He appears to have been a competent designer, and his work reflected well the taste of his period. He was, in fact, the only Canadian to be mentioned in the International Exhibition of 1893.

In 1898, while in his forties, Robert McCausland was commissioned, with architect E.J. Lennox, to create a window for the stairwell of the Toronto City Hall which was then being built. The result, one of the largest stained-glass windows on the continent, is a splendid example of Canada's artistic aspirations at the turn of the century.

The theme of the work – The Union of Commerce and Industry – is interpreted in Canadian terms. In the background there is a view of the City Hall being built. And beyond that there is a realistic representation of the Toronto waterfront, complete with sailing ships and steamships. The St. Lawrence Hall can be seen, flying a very controversial flag – the first approved red ensign, which had the coats of arms of seven provinces in a maple leaf circle. (It was this insignia, favoured by John A. Macdonald, which caused some incidents between Canada and the United Kingdom in the late 1800's. The Royal Navy, which objected to its use, regularly confiscated it and fined the ship-owners concerned.)

The window depicts artisans going about their business, and is embellished with allegorical figures representing the Continents, Industry and Commerce. To complete the composition there is a glorious sun, symbolizing prosperity.

Lennox and McCausland collaborated on a number of other commissions, including a mausoleum for the Massey family, windows for the King Edward Hotel in Toronto, and a conservatory dome for Sir Henry Pellatt's home, *Casa Loma,* also in Toronto. Eventually, however, they quarrelled over the installation of a window in St. Paul's Church, Toronto. McCausland believed that the window would be affected by condensation. Lennox disagreed. There *was* condensation, however, and another window had to be installed on the outside to correct the problem. McCausland had it done and sent the bill to Lennox, who refused to pay. For six years the matter hung fire. Finally, on the eve of a lawsuit, Lennox paid. But there were no further collaborations.

There are few towns in Canada that don't have some of the McCausland designs, though not all of them are signed. He accepted commissions from all across the country,

Stained glass window done by Robert McCausland 1898 for Toronto City Hall

and produced a great quantity of stained glass for churches, homes, and other buildings.

At the present time there are a number of gifted Canadian artists working with stained glass, even though commissions are very limited because of the high costs involved, and despite the fact that supplies are often difficult to obtain. Almost all of them are using the traditional techniques – painstakingly leading together hand-cut pieces of pre-coloured glass.

The stained-glass windows in the House of Commons which depict the flower emblems of all the provinces are good examples of the work currently being done. Each window is made up of 2500 pieces of glass, and the effect when the sun shines through into the dignified gloom of the Chamber is truly spectacular.

Knitting & Knotting

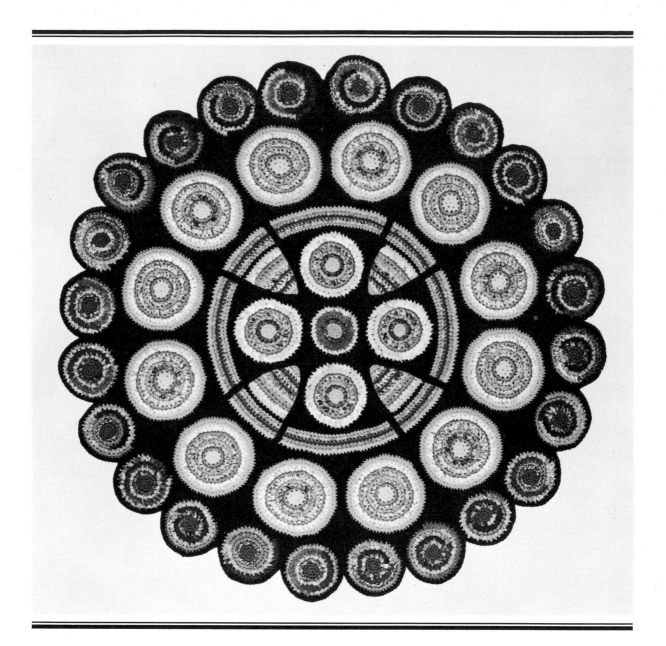

Crocheted wall panel by Germaine Garneau, Pont-Viau, Quebec.

Knitting

It is thought that the first people to knit were North African nomads and Arab traders, and that during their wanderings they carried the craft into Tibet and eventually into the Mediterranean area. From there it spread throughout the world, no doubt because it is ideal pick-up work for travellers and shepherds – indeed for all those whose hands would otherwise be idle.

Arab camel drivers knitted as they crossed the endless stretches of sand. Sailors knitted as they whiled away the long watches. And English coachmen knitted as they traversed the lonely hills – holding a long needle with a curved handle firmly pressed to their body with one elbow, and manipulating the wool with another short needle. (This left them one hand free for the reins.)

The Arabs were proficient knitters; they used not only straight needles but circular ones for tubular articles. And they used a pegged frame in the same way children later used spools circled with tacks for corkwork. They also had a fine sense of colour and design, and this too they transmitted to the people with whom they came in contact. The Spaniards, in particular, became very skilful in executing intricate patterns, and legend has it that it was from the Spanish Armada sailors shipwrecked on their shores that the knitters of Fair Isle acquired their distinctive style.

In most parts of Europe knitting was, for some time, done with natural-coloured wool, and it was fashionable to make it look as much like textile as possible. To this end the wool was felted by soaking and pummelling it so that the fabric tightened and shrank until all signs of stitches were obliterated.

When silken yarn was introduced, it became fashionable to simulate brocade and embossed materials. Colour became an important feature, and high relief patterns were popular.

Gold and silver metal threads were sometimes combined with the silk. They protected the more perishable yarn because, being thicker, they took most of the rub. And they added a touch of luxury, which made them particularly suitable for ecclesiastical trappings such as bishops' gloves.

The introduction of coloured yarns and varied weaves gave an impetus to knitting. Every country, every town developed its own unique styles and designs. Fishermen from the west coast ports of England and Ireland could easily be identified by their sweater patterns, which usually bore names closely associated with the Bible – names like Star of Bethlehem, Sacred Crown and Crown of Glory.

Professional knitters set up shop, producing throws and rugs as well as sweaters, hats, stockings, gloves and other garments. High standards of workmanship were maintained by the formation of hosiery guilds that demanded rigid training of young apprentices. The professional knitters were always men; indeed knitting was, for the most part, a masculine occupation at that time.

By the time the first settlers came to Canada, knitting had become a household tradition. A great deal of it was done here because knitwear was warm yet light-weight – ideal for the climate. In the early days, when wool was scarce, worn garments were unravelled, and the wool was washed, stretched and reknitted.

In Canada, unlike the Old Country, the men of the family did not knit; they were too occupied with the heavy tasks involved in getting established in a new land. The women did most of the knitting; but it was considered a very suitable occupation for children, especially for boys who might otherwise be engaged in time-wasting or mischievous pursuits. In her book *The American Frugal Housewife,* published in New York in 1838, Mrs. Child said:

"A child of six years old can be made useful; and should be taught to consider every day lost on which some useful little thing has not been done to assist others. Children can be very early taught to tackle all the care of their own clothes. They can knit garters, suspenders and stockings; they can make patchwork and braid straw; they can make mats for the table, and mats for the floor; they can weed the garden and pick cranberries from the meadow to be carried to market."

When times became easier the boys of the family ceased to knit, but the women continued; they found it pleasant leisure-time work and became skilled in reproducing intricate patterns. They made shawls, bed covers and lacy curtains. They made rugs by looping strips of cloth into a knitted background, and knitted beads into the fabric of garments and handbags. Beaded bags, popular around the end of the nineteenth century, were made from patterns in the women's magazines which supplied stitch-by-stitch directions for producing elaborate floral designs.

48

BASIC KNITTING STITCHES

CASTING ON

GARTER STITCH

PURL

BINDING OFF

"La Dame Blanche," masque wall hanging by
Louise Riopel Hamel, Longueuil, Quebec

Macramé wall hanging by Sue Scott, Ottawa,
Ontario*

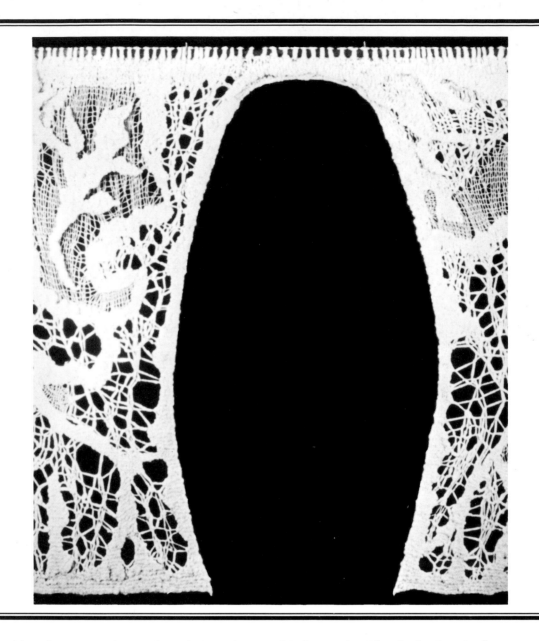

Knitted handspun wool, "Arch with Gryphon and Salamander," by Catherine Anderson, Summerland, British Columbia*

Long before the settlers arrived, the Indians were knitting. It is generally held that they developed the art of finger knitting before they had any contact with the white man, but that they acquired the knowledge of knitting with needles from the early explorers and fur traders. This theory is borne out by the fact that the Indians of the coastal regions are particularly adept at it.

To this day the Cowichan Indian women of British Columbia are noted for the beautiful sweaters they make. They select black and white fleeces which they hand wash, card and spin, blending some of the wool in the process to produce grey and brown shades. The yarn is then knitted according to patterns that have been handed down from generation to generation in the family or group. Some patterns are abstract, others are based on animal forms. There is a strong resemblance between Cowichan designs and those of the Fair Isle knitters, and historians have concluded that the Scottish employees of the Hudson's Bay Company must have taught the Indians their traditional patterns.

The Eskimos too, are skilled knitters, though they apparently had no knowledge of the craft before the white man appeared on the scene. They obtain their fibre by collecting the wisps of wild musk ox wool that cling to the bushes and rocks, and they spin it in much the same way as they make thread from sinew – by twisting and plying two threads with the fingers.

Nowadays some Eskimos also spin and knit the wool of the domesticated musk ox, the quiviut.

In the 1930's a herd of wild musk ox were brought from Greenland and introduced into Nunivak Island in the Bering Sea. They thrived, and have become the source of a new industry. Encouraged by white craftsmen, the Eskimos have learned to collect the soft underhair of the musk ox in the spring, easing it through the long guard hairs on the animal's back with their fingers. The down, which forms a lightly curled mass like a giant powder puff, requires no carding and has little grease or debris. In its natural state it is grey-brown, but it dyes well, never matting even when stirred in hot water. It is easily spun, and the finished fibre combines the softness of angora with the toughness of sheep's wool.

The processing of the quiviut down combines new and old techniques. The fibre is machine-spun but the yarn is hand-knitted. The knitters work as individuals, but the finished articles are marketed co-operatively.

51

A few of the many knitting patterns:

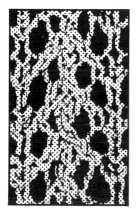
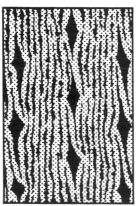

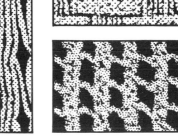

C. Basket weave

D. Honeycomb

A. Allover lace   B. Eyelet

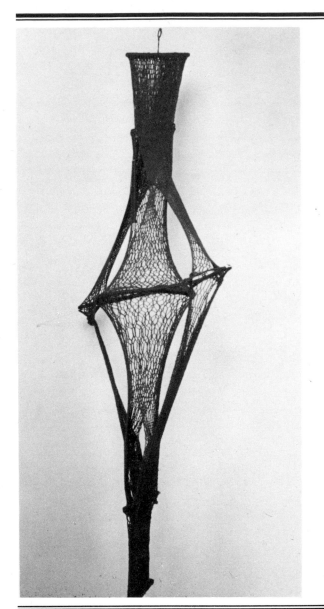

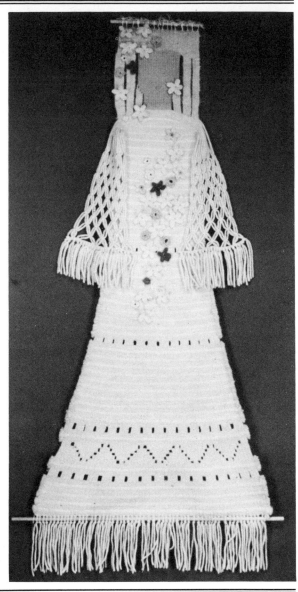

*Sprang hanging by Marie Aiken,
Gravenhurst, Ontario**

*"Ophelia," macramé and woven wall
hanging by Nina Jursevskis, Toronto, Ontario*

The hoods, scarves, mitts and socks made from musk ox wool are very light and soft, yet warm. They are scarce as yet, however, and expensive.

The knitters of today are breaking new ground in their approach to the craft. It has become a form of self-expression, rather than a pastime or useful occupation. Colour is being used in a more adventurous way. Substances other than wool, silk or cotton (rope, string, ribbon, plastic and even horsehair) are being utilized. And there is an increasing tendency to incorporate structural supports or wadding to produce three-dimensional objects. The creative knitter has turned his back on prescribed designs and is venturing into new territory, influenced by the bold, uncluttered feel of contemporary art.

Crocheting

The craft of crocheting probably originated – or at least was perfected – during the mediaeval period, when nuns in convents used it to decorate vestments and altar cloths. It was then called "nuns' work," and it is thought that original crochet patterns spread from one convent to another as the nuns moved about. The convent pupils, who were taught to crochet, carried the craft to the secular world, and it became a cottage industry, practised by all members of the family.

The second great crochet period took place in Ireland in the mid-nineteenth century when Irish lace (which is not, properly speaking, lace at all) was developed to imitate the expensive Venetian lace. Introduced during the Great Famine of 1845-47, Irish lace became popular because it could be produced in the home and required no investment apart from a hook and a ball of twine, which society ladies supplied as an act of charity. It was also relatively simple to make, consisting merely of tightly crocheted medallions – or birds, or flowers – which were joined together with a crocheted web.

During the first quarter of the twentieth century a second crochet revival took place in the United States and Canada. At that time heavy yarns were introduced, and many people found it much more satisfying to work with this new material which bulked up quickly and looked impressive. It was particularly suitable for bedspreads, curtains, tablecloths, antimacassars and throws, and for some years most homes were cluttered with crocheted articles of all kinds.

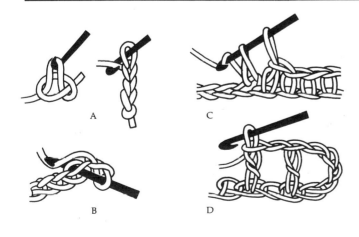

The basic crochet stitches are: A. Chain stitch (shown also in detail), B. Single crochet, and C. Variation of single crochet, D. Open or filet mesh. These are elementary but extremely useful.

Hanging fibre sculpture by Hilde Schreier, Ottawa, Ontario*

Another revival began in the 1950's. This time crocheted clothing became popular, and many garments that had previously been knitted or woven were crocheted. The trend is still very much in evidence.

In the late 1960's craftsmen, spurred on by the invention of larger tools, the use of less conventional materials, and the general tendency to shake off old traditions, began to take crocheting out of the fashion and household category and to experiment with it as an art form.

One manifestation of this was that crochet began to take on some of the aspects of sculpture; stuffing and structural supports were sometimes incorporated into the fabric to produce three-dimensional articles.

Crocheting, like knitting, has now become as much a creative art as a utilitarian craft. Pieces are made for purely decorative purposes, and hangings of crochet work, or crochet combined with knitting or macramé, are often found in galleries and public buildings.

Macramé

Out of utility comes art. As appliqué evolved from the homely patch, so macramé developed from a simple knotting operation done with the fingers. There are two basic knots — the flat, or reef knot, and the half-hitch. In the most basic pieces twine is braided and knotted longitudinally to make a mesh. More complicated pieces involve variations of the knots, the introduction of horizontal fibres, and changes in tension. The resulting fabric resembles three-dimensional lace and affords an intriguing interplay of light and shadow.

As a knotting craft macramé has a long and varied history. It is believed that it originated in the Middle East. Certainly the geometric patterns have an affinity with Arabic design, and the name itself is derived from the Arabic word for head shawl. The craft was probably taken to Europe by the Crusaders, and became particularly popular in Moorish Spain, where all manner of macramé articles were made, from belts to shawls. From there it spread to the Riviera coast as far as Genoa. There was so much interest in the craft that for hundreds of years the skill was taught to boys and girls in convent schools. Some of these pupils became professional macramé workers and their creations were exported to South America and California.

Solomon's knot, #3, one of the basic macramé knots, is like a reef knot but is tied around two central threads. With variations of this and the half hitch and overhand knots (#1 and #2), intricate meshes that serve both useful and decorative purposes can be made. Usually the threads are attached to a foundation bar which is removed when the mesh is completed.

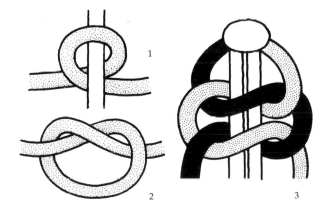

The Spaniards, in turn, introduced macramé into Mexico, where it is known as Mexican lace. During their occupation of the Netherlands they spread the art in that country. And then Queen Mary, the wife of William of Orange, took it to England where it became a popular upper-class pastime for many years. It was especially favoured at court because it was a suitable activity for idle hands in the evenings when poor lighting made fine needlework impossible.

There is another theory that macramé was spread by sailors who were old hands at tying functional knots. The decorative knotting developed from the fact that, unless a crisis occurred, half the crew was able to rest while the remainder kept watch. During these leisure hours the sailors, in their restricted quarters, occupied themselves doing what they knew best – knotting and sewing. Macramé articles were easy to pack into their bags, to be sold or given away in port. In addition, the ship was the sailor's home and he loved to decorate it. Knotted fringes were made to cover the bells and sometimes knotted screens were erected so that the ankles of women passengers were not immodestly exposed when they were climbing ladders. Seamen, of course, didn't use the word "macramé"; they called it "square knotting" or "McNamara's lace."

Canadian Indians were adept at macramé, which they learned from the sailors. Those on the east coast made belts, garters and bands, using strips of cedar bark, basswood fibre, deer sinews, string and rawhide (babiche). The tribes living in Quebec used a combination of finger weaving and knotting to make decorative sashes similar to the ceintures fléchées worn by the habitants. Other tribes made robes from rabbit skins that were cut into strips, rolled and knotted, the knots worked so closely together that the fur covered the holes. In fact, today some of the Indians of northern Ontario and Manitoba still make rabbit skin hats in this way, with the fur on both the inside and the outside.

Macramé has continued to be widely practised in the Mediterranean countries, but in the northern countries its popularity has waxed and waned. In the nineteenth century there was a revival of interest in the craft when fashion decreed the embellishment of everything from shawls to household linen, and it enjoyed popularity into the twentieth century. It faded into virtual obscurity during the thirties, however, when dress and decoration became austere and stark. The 1960's saw yet another revival, and for the first time the trend was to use it as an end in itself rather than as an applied decoration. It is now more apt to appear as a wall hanging, a sculpture, a belt, a piece of jewellery, a plant

Macramé wedding veil by Beverley Williams, Whitby, Ontario

Irish lace collar, early twentieth century (Royal Ontario Museum)

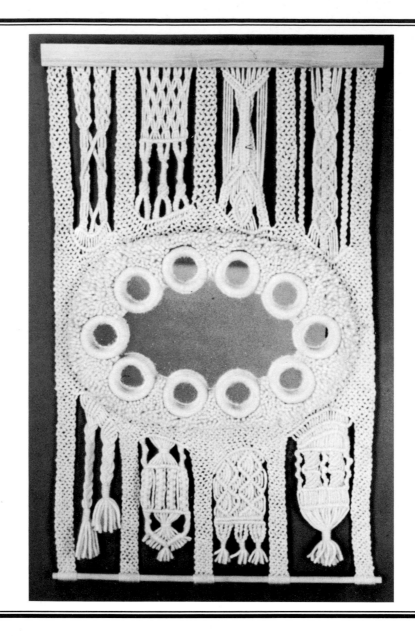

"Swan Lake," macramé wall hanging, by Linda Sirr McAleenan, Willowdale, Ontario

holder, or a satchel – constructed of either the traditional fibres of linen, cotton, rope, twine, and hemp, or contemporary fibres, including translucent plastic film.

Lace-making & Tatting

Lace is an opened-patterned fabric made by looping, twisting or weaving fine thread. In the case of hand-made lace, the thread is usually linen or silk, but occasionally gold or silver. In the case of machine-made lace, the thread is generally cotton.

There are only two ways to make lace by hand – with a bobbin or with a needle. The bobbin, a form of shuttle, is used to weave and knot the thread which, for convenience's sake, is anchored to a stiff pillow. The needle is used to reinforce material from which threads have been drawn to create an open pattern. This type of lacework varies all the way from simple hemstitching to elaborate drawn-work in which geometric, flower and animal motifs are featured, and sometimes embroidered.

The art of making lace evolved in western Europe around the end of the fifteenth century, and reached its height in Italy and Flanders during the next hundred years. It was given impetus by the publication of pattern books which, like cookbooks and fables, were considered "safe" at a time when it was dangerous to publish books on controversial or anti-clerical subjects.

It was during this period too that the demand for lace was at its peak. Gentlemen wore shirts with billowing lace cuffs, and ladies wore gowns elaborately trimmed with it. Churchmen wore lace on their neck-pieces, and servants wore it on their uniforms. Great quantities of lace were also required for household linens and furnishings of all kinds.

Once the demand began to dwindle, however, the workmanship deteriorated, and though hand-made lace was available for the next two hundred years, the craft never again achieved the position of preeminence that it enjoyed during the sixteenth century. In time it came to be little more than a pastime for wealthy women or a tedious task for the few who continued to produce lace for the market.

Eventually, in the eighteenth century, the cottage industry was forced completely out of existence by machine-made lace. Machines could copy accurately almost any pattern, and lace, once the prerogative of the wealthy, was now available to all. And so a new lace era came into being. Machine-made lace trimmed everything from egg-cosy covers to

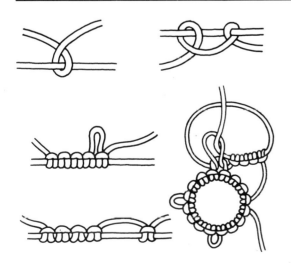

Tatting is made by looping and knotting thread over thread with a shuttle. The basic stitch consists of two halves of a knot, one made under the thread and one over. When a number of knots have been made the thread is pulled to form a ring. Loops, or picots, are made periodically to give the work a lacy look. Chains are also made in this way, of two threads rather than one.

undergarments. It positively smothered nineteenth-century babies.

In North America lace-making never became an important craft. In the days of settlement most housewives were too busy to engage in such a time-consuming pursuit, and though many of them had been taught the art in the Old Country it was gradually forgotten except in convents and in wealthy households. Today it is seldom practised except by women of European birth, and the patterns and techniques employed are the traditional ones they learned in their homelands.

Tatting, which takes its name from "tatters," meaning "fragile," is a very ancient form of lace-making done by looping and knotting threads with the help of a shuttle. Practised from early times by the Chinese and Egyptians, the art spread to Europe, where it reached a peak during the early eighteenth century. It then declined, but was revived in the mid-nineteenth century, that heyday of pick-up work.

It is thought that Mary of Orange, who was famous for her magnificent tatting, contributed to the rise of the art during the late seventeenth century. And it was another queen – Marie of Roumania – who kept it alive during the early part of the twentieth century when very little tatting was being done. Queen Marie was especially noted for the work she did for religious vestments and church linens, and was among the first to develop a method of working precious and semi-precious stones into the lace.

Today tatting is being revived, but Canadian craftsmen are now diverting it from its original use as an edging for garments and household linens to more spectacular service. It is, for example, often used as a component in fabric collage and frequently appears as an element in woven tapestry and crochet sculpture.

The materials too are different now. The traditional silk, cotton and linen are being replaced by metal, plastic, string, wool and straw – indeed by anything that will wind on a shuttle. Obviously, the revolution in the creative crafts, which has so far largely by-passed lace-making, has taken tatting into its orbit.

Leatherwork

Leather was one of the first materials to be used by man as protection against the cold and against the weapons of his enemies. Since then it has served many purposes. It has been used for tents, armour, food containers, drinking cups, saddles, furniture, reliquaries, masks, toys, windowpanes, sails, and many other things – including clothing and footwear.

In the beginning hides were not tanned, and as a result they were stiff, strong-smelling and perishable. But then prehistoric man began to improve the skins. He scraped them to remove the hair and particles of flesh, beat them and pounded in oil and grease to soften them, and finally stretched them. Later it was discovered that if the skins were treated with salt and then soaked, with oak bark, in a water-filled pit, they became soft and durable. After that the tanning process became a standard step in the preparation of most leather. Untanned skins were still used to some extent, however, since they were particularly suited for certain purposes; rawhide, which was waterproof and tough, was used principally for heavy-duty luggage, and parchment was used for letters and manuscripts.

It is believed that the practice of decorating leather by tooling it originated in the Near East, was transmitted into Spain by the Moors, and spread from there to Italy. In due course it was taken to Mexico by the Spanish *conquistadores* and there it has been practised with great skill ever since.

It was in Italy, however, that the tooling of leather was carried to great heights. From the twelfth century on craftsmen there produced leatherwork that was extremely sophisticated. They pressed designs into it, embossed it by tooling the underside, carved it very much as wood is carved, burned patterns into the surface, and did intricate inlay work. They also shaped leather by boiling it and stamping it in a mould. And they made objects out of scrap leather using the papier-mâché technique.

Fancy articles of all kinds were made with tooled leather. Writing cases, containers for eating utensils (a must for all travellers), book covers, jewel cases, and satchels were just a few of the luxury items produced by Italian craftsmen. They also covered carved wooden boxes with leather, tamping the fabric well down into the recesses to produce the effect of high relief.

Gradually the art of working leather spread throughout Europe, and leather objects began to appear in even modest homes. A major breakthrough in the treating of hides

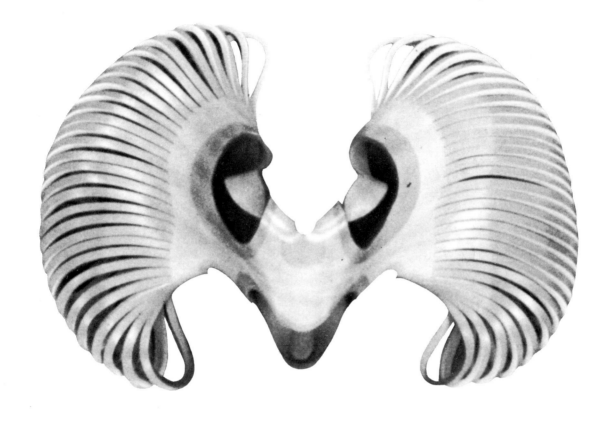

Leather mask by Rex Lingwood, Schomberg, Ontario

Leather chess set by Paul Williams, Whitby, Ontario

Cuir-bouilli *jugs by Robert Muma, Toronto, Ontario. (For these the leather was soaked, stretched on wooden moulds, then baked in an oven at 225°F.)*

took place early in the nineteenth century when the English chemist Sir Humphry Davy discovered that the bark of the hemlock, chestnut and mimosa would serve as well in the tanning operation as that of the oak. This was followed by the introduction of a new tanning process based on the use of chrome salts. It was a quicker method and it produced a finer grade of leather. As a result there was a sharp increase in the manufacturing of leather goods. Factory-made boots, shoes, boxes, purses and other leather articles were turned out in great abundance, and – inevitably – the craftsman was crowded off the stage.

The Indians and Eskimos of North America were very skilled in their handling of animal skins, which they used extensively for clothing, shelter, shields and containers of all kinds, and which they traded from tribe to tribe.

In some areas the Indians practised a form of tanning; they pounded oil and animal brains into the scraped hides, then left them hanging in heavy smoke. Buckskin was produced in this way, from deerhide. In other areas they simply scraped the skins and softened them by pulling them back and forth around a stake. Rawhide was used a great deal, however, even in the regions where skins were tanned. Rattles, drums and boxes were made of it. So were parflèches – large envelopes in which dried berries, pemmican and corn were packed. And rawhide thongs were cut for snowshoe webbing and fishnets.

Many of the eastern and central tribes decorated their leather with quillwork, moosehair or shells. The Naskapi of the Quebec-Labrador peninsula trimmed their full-skirted coat with colourful painted borders.

The Eskimos too decorated their garments with appliqué and embroidery. The hides were not tanned but were chewed to suppleness by the women, who wore down their teeth in the process. The clothing was skilfully made and was warm, since the fur side was generally worn next to the body.

The early traders and settlers obtained hides from the Indians for their own use as well as for export. Many of them also adopted the Indian style of dress, since they found it admirably suited to the climate and mode of life.

As settlement progressed, however, the white people began to make their own leather garments, saddlery and footwear. They fashioned their boots with little wooden pegs rather than with stitching because they found that the dampness caused sinews to stretch and rot. And they made both shoes exactly the same. (Colonial boot-makers did not adopt the refinement of right and left shaping until well into the nineteenth century. Until then men in the army were required to switch boots from foot to foot every few days so that they would wear evenly.)

Eventually commercial tanneries were established in the larger communities – always beside a river or lake, since water was required for the various processes. They supplied dressed leather to the settlers, the itinerant boot-makers and later to the factories that took over the manufacturing of leather goods. They also sold to the carriage-makers when they began operating in Canada. The carriage-makers were important customers, since they used leather for the interiors, the roofs and sometimes for the outside of their vehicles as well.

The rise of industry heralded the decline of hand-done leatherwork, however. It was not until the 1960's that the craft was revived, and the potential of the medium remains largely unrealized.

Today the most creative work is being done by craftsmen who are experimenting with new techniques. They are weaving and knotting leather, appliquéing and batiking it, and using it to make clothing, furniture, jewellery, chess sets, sculpture, and decorative objects of all kinds.

Bookbinding

Despite the fact that mass-produced books are now readily available and comparatively cheap there is today a revival of the ancient craft of making books. These craftsmen, instead of competing with the volume of commercial book printers, turn their skills to producing small editions over which they have total control. In some instances the paper, type, ink, illustrations and binding are considered not separate operations but aspects of a single, co-ordinated craft. In other cases the craftsman specializes in one particular area: he may make paper using a linen and rag base, cut wood blocks for illustrations, set type by hand, print manually, or sew and bind printed sheets.

Of these various operations paper-making has been the most recent development. Although from ancient times words were preserved on stone, clay, parchment, horn and papyrus, the manufacture of paper as we know it was not introduced until the second century. At that time the Chinese discovered that the inner bark of the mulberry could be

Examples of hand-bound and hand-printed books from the Toronto Public Library Collection.
Also leather-covered books hand-bound by Michael Wilcox of Woodview, Ontario

pounded and pressed into sheets. Later they found that the addition of rags improved the quality of the paper.

This method of manufacture spread to the West when Chinese papermakers were captured in battle by the Arabs. The Moors carried the art to Spain and the Crusaders brought it into northern Europe. Subsequently many improvements were made in the process, one of the most important being the development of a machine to make paper on rolls. From that point the manufacture of paper became a commercial operation, and hand-made paper practically disappeared from the market. It was not until recent years that the craft was revived, when some people interested in typography and discontent with the quality of mass-produced paper, began to return to the old method of manufacture. Even today the production of hand-made paper is rare and specialized. The principal practitioners of the craft at the present time are the Japanese who never allowed it to die completely.

Today there is also a revival of the ancient art of manuscript illumination which reached great heights at the end of the Dark Ages. Then the Church and the nobility vied with each other to commission handwritten manuscripts embellished with elaborate letters and scenes painted in gold, silver and bright colours. Many of these were of unsurpassed beauty. Even today, seven hundred years later, the illustrations glow with their original light. The basis of the colouring in the manuscripts was egg white mixed with natural pigments from finely ground precious metals, materials still used by illuminators.

Canada has produced some exquisite modern examples of this craft, mainly among the commissioned books of remembrance created to honour those who died in World Wars I and II.

Some hand-made books are being illustrated with pictures reproduced in the old fashion. Blocks of wood, stone or metal are cut by hand in the traditional manner: all but the portions to be inked are excised. Even the impressing is done by hand, and interesting variations are achieved by fluctuations in inking and pressure.

The printing of the text is also occasionally done by hand for books produced in limited editions. These are generally hand-sewn, and bound according to a method that has been perfected from early times. Indeed, bookbinding as a newly-revived craft is being practised extensively in Europe and more recently in Canada by European trained craftsmen.

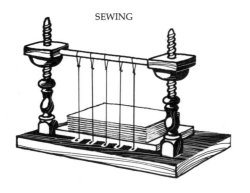

SEWING

There are eight basic steps in the hand binding of books: The sheets are sewn together in signatures (8, 16 or 32 pages). The signatures are collated, placed in a frame and sewn to cords. The sewn book is clamped between boards and the pages trimmed. The back is rounded. Stiff cardboards are attached to the cords. These are covered with leather, cloth or paper. The endpapers are pasted on the inside of the covers. The book is tied firmly in a brace to dry.

It was not until commercial binderies became common in the nineteenth century that the custom of binding paperback books by hand to protect them went out of common practice. Even today, in France, it is usual to buy books in paper covers and then take those with lasting value to a bookbinder to be re-bound in more durable covers.

There have been bookbinders in Canada since the eighteenth century. In New France the craft was sponsored by the Church and even today some convents do custom bookbinding. The Maritime craftsmen, who were mostly Loyalists, produced work comparable to that of the European bookbinders, an achievement which pleased their customers, who were from the carriage class. In all parts of the country both customers and craftsmen adhered to the traditional bindings of their homelands. In Upper Canada the Mennonites had their Bibles, prayer-books and hymn-books bound in the German manner with heavy leather, ornate tooling, and highly-coloured endpapers.

In nineteenth-century Canada the LaFrance and the Lemieux families were famous for their bookbinding. The LaFrance family included four bookbinding brothers who carried their trade into Toronto and Ottawa. The Lemieux family worked throughout the nineteenth century and a descendant, Marguerite Lemieux, was binding – and signing – her work in the twentieth century. She applied coloured leathers in the modern French manner, and examples of her work are now collectors' items.

Custom bookbinders today work in the traditional way. Groups of signatures (sixteen-page sections) are sewn together, glued and compressed. The sewn pages are then fastened into a hard cover which consists of heavy cardboard covered with leather, paper or cloth. Leather-bound books are hand-decorated with tooling and stamping.

Custom bookbinders are flourishing in Canada at the present time. The majority bind fine books conservatively, but more and more collectors are encouraging them to bind in a contemporary style.

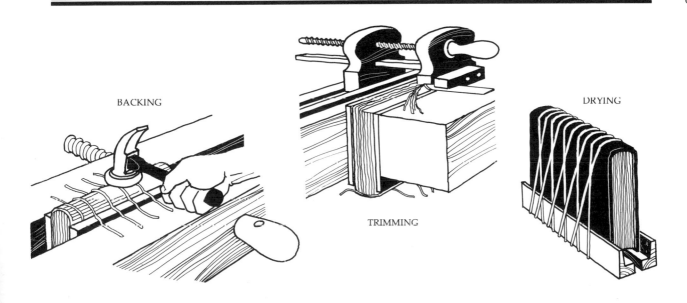

BACKING

TRIMMING

DRYING

Metalwork

The history of the world is measured in terms of metal. The four ages of classical mythology were named for gold, silver, bronze and iron, and similar labels are used to designate specific stages of man's technological and cultural development. The association is natural; metal has played an important part in the daily life of the human race for thousands of years. It has been used for coinage, jewellery, construction, furniture, household wares, coffers – for a whole host of things. And the list grows constantly.

The working of metals began in prehistoric times, when it was discovered that some metals (notably copper and lead) would melt, and that they could be moulded and hammered. From that time on rapid progress was made. At an early date tin was being alloyed with copper to make bronze, and by 2000 B.C. the Egyptians had accomplished the difficult task of separating iron from its ore. Further advances were made during the Middle Ages when alchemists, searching for a way to make gold, stumbled upon some very important facts about metals and their behaviour.

The processing of metals had an important effect on world trade. The possessors of tin and copper, for example, traded it to the people of Spain, England and Ireland in exchange for bronze. The bronze was bartered for jet, amber and other stones which were used to enhance the metalwork. And the search for additional sources of mineral wealth opened up new territory and new markets.

Trade, in turn, affected the development of metallurgy. There was an exchange of information as well as goods, and as a result many techniques came to be relatively standard all over the world. To this day craftsmen everywhere forge and hammer metal to shape it and give it tension. Everywhere they use the same procedures in moulding and casting.

For example, craftsmen are still using the old "lost wax" method of casting in which a wax model of an object is covered with a plaster-clay mixture. The wax is then melted out and molten metal is poured into the hollow. An even older technique, sand casting (similar to the method described in Glass-making), is also widely practised, though it does not give the best results as far as delineation of detail is concerned. (There is a new method of casting, however – electro-forming – in which a base – usually styrofoam – is covered with electrodeposited metal. This procedure is gaining acceptance as well.)

Similar methods of decorating metal are also practised the world over. Gold and silver, for example, are ornamented by repoussé, in which the detail is pushed out from the back

Sterling silver tumbler with 18K. gold by Michael T. Wolf, Delta, British Columbia

"The Two Gentlemen of Verona," ebony and silver pendant by Pat Hunt, Don Mills, Ontario

Silver tea caddy made in mid-nineteenth century by Michael Septimus Brown, Halifax, Nova Scotia

Sterling silver perfume bottle by Marc André Beaudin, Quebec*

Silver and enamel bowl by Yves and Micheline de Passillé-Sylvestre, Ste Adele en Haut, Quebec

Silver and enamel chalice by Donald A. Stuart, Barrie, Ontario

with punches; and by chasing, a refinement of repoussé in which the work is turned to the front and the final detail is applied with chasing tools to give a depth to the design.

Gold and silver may also be embellished with cloisonné which is basically a design formed from fine wire soldered to a base. Enamel powder is placed in the design and the piece is fired. The metal doesn't melt but the enamel turns to glass. The Chinese and Japanese are supreme masters of the art of cloisonné, which is being practised by an increasing number of craftsmen today.

Enamelling, which can be done on all metals, was known to the Byzantines who considered such work as precious as jewels, and used it not only for personal jewellery but for decorating churches and public buildings (often pictorially for the instruction of the illiterate). Enamelling reached great heights in Europe during the Celtic and Anglo-Saxon cultures. A piece made for Alfred the Great, which included green leaves on a white ground set in a pebble-finished red gold, was a very splendid example of the extremely sophisticated pieces being made extensively at that time. Later, in the fifteenth century, artisans at Limoges learned to superimpose one layer of enamel over another.

Enamelling was revived in the late eighteenth century when English craftsmen produced pastoral scenes on boxes, mirror frames and lamp bases, using a white ground. Another revival came in the mid-nineteenth century when the work of Fabergé was at its height. One of the finest goldsmiths and enamellists of all times, Fabergé had made an extensive study of ancient Chinese, Greek and Russian metalwork. He was a pioneer in the *Art Nouveau* movement, and a flamboyant craftsman, hypnotized by the colours of gold and the variations of enamel.

Today the tendency among metal workers is to return to old techniques, many of which have fallen into disuse. They are, for example, joining metals not only by soldering and welding them but by means of the lost art of granulation, which was developed by the Assyrians and Greeks. This method is based on the discovery that when two pieces of metal are heated the molecules of both surfaces interchange and lock together.

Jewellery, utensils, implements, grill work, woven hangings, plaques, and numerous other objects are being crafted out of metal at the present time. Gold, silver, copper, pewter, steel, iron and aluminum are all being worked, individually or in combination, and are being finished with enamelling, cloisonné, hammering and etching. "Found" objects such as stones, seeds, beads, plastics and wood are frequently incorporated.

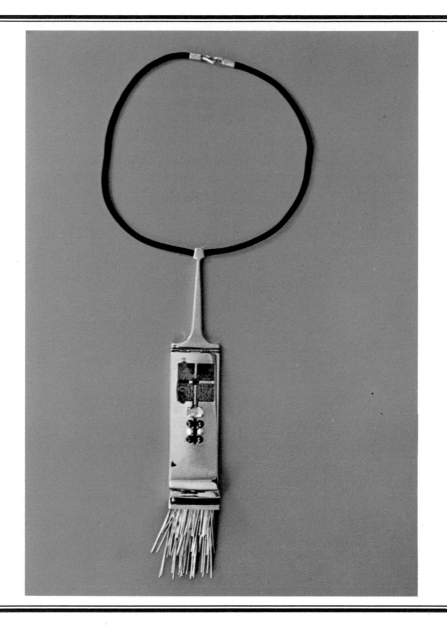

*Sterling silver neckpiece, fire gilded, with pearls and moonstone, by Haakon Bakken, Mississauga, Ontario**

Techniques and trends vary from metal to metal, however, and each medium should therefore be considered individually.

Iron

The great advantage of iron is its cheapness, abundance and widespread availability. It was first worked in the Middle East about 3000 B.C. when sickle blades, ploughs and other tools were hammered out of iron obtained from fallen meteors. It was first mined in Asia about 1000 B.C., and not long after mines were being worked in Africa and Europe. The inhabitants of southern Europe knew and used the metal long before the northerners, but the British and Scandinavians, though they came late to the trade, became adept at it. The Vikings, in particular, made very sophisticated objects of iron, and at present there is a theory that they taught some of the North American Indians with whom they came in contact how to process and utilize the metal.

The working of iron eventually spawned many allied crafts. Armourers, gunsmiths, locksmiths, and even safe-makers all owe their craft to the first iron workers.

In the New World settlers very soon began to process their own iron, to make essential tools and objects. Their work was made easier by the fact that bog iron was available. This did not have to be mined, but could be taken from the surface of marshy areas and processed fairly simply.

The first foundry in this country – the St. Maurice works – was established in 1735 at Trois Rivières. For a hundred years it made iron hollowware, stoves and cannon. In the meantime, of course, other foundries had been set up and by that time settlers were able to buy axes, cooking pots, fire irons and boilers. Eventually some foundries specialized; they made bathtubs, furniture, ornaments and kitchen utensils. In addition, every village had its blacksmith who shoed the oxen and horses, and also made more complicated objects such as latches, locks, and tombstone railings, according to his ability.

By mid-century there was an overlap; commercial ironworks were producing articles similar to those turned out by the blacksmith. For some time the craftsman held his own by making individually designed objects. But mass production couldn't be halted, and the introduction of blast furnaces spelled the end of the village smithy. The new foundries could cast and stamp almost everything, from traditional work to intricate pieces which

76

WROUGHT IRON FITTINGS

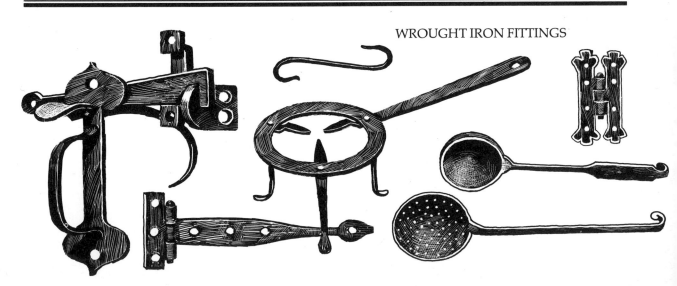

the blacksmith couldn't copy.

A few craftsmen continued to work, usually in isolated areas or because they had some special area of expertise, such as gunsmithing. But in general the smith limited himself to shoeing horses and oxen, mending ploughshares, and occasionally removing with his tongs the aching tooth of a neighbour.

Iron has been rediscovered of recent years because it has structural strength which limits the use of other, softer metals in the making of large objects. But contemporary ironworkers, many of whom have experience in working with gold or silver or in sculpturing, are combining the metal with brass, glass, copper and gold. They have also discovered that it can be drawn, formed, machined, etched and coloured. But when it is white hot it is very plastic, and must be worked with great speed and a sure eye for design and form. It therefore presents a challenge to the craftsman who is concerned with making the most of its versatility.

Copper

Objects of copper have been found among the remains of early civilizations of China, Asia and the Mediterranean world, so we know that it has been crafted for a very long time – some say from the very beginning of metalworking. Perhaps this is because it is an easy metal to work; it can be readily beaten into shape. It is also a good conductor of heat and has been used from early times for cooking pots – though the pots have to be lined with another metal since poisonous copper salts form on the surface, particularly in the presence of acids.

Because copper does not corrode it was at one time used to sheathe the hulls of wooden ships. For the same reason, as well as because it is decorative, it has been widely used for doors, roofs, weather vanes, and trim on buildings.

Copper can also be easily engraved. It has therefore been one of the basic metals for coinage and has played an important role in the printing of pictures on paper and textiles. It is believed that this printing process was invented by a fifteenth-century Florentine coppersmith who discovered that by incising metal to leave decorative lines in relief, and filling in the recesses with ink, he could reproduce the design on other substances.

In North America copper was being worked by the Indians before the arrival of the

white man. Cartier's interest was aroused when he saw that the St. Lawrence Indians had some of the metal in their possession and later travellers, including Brûlé and Radisson, mentioned that the natives had copper nuggets and ornaments. In 1665 a search revealed a number of large deposits on the south shore of Lake Superior and in 1734 mining operations were begun there. They were brought to a halt, however, when trouble arose with the Indians. The search for copper was also one of the purposes behind Samuel Hearne's epoch-making journey to the mouth of the Coppermine River in 1771-2.

The Indians in the eastern part of Canada used copper, particularly that from the Lake Superior area, turning it into weapons, implements and utensils. On the west coast some tribes obtained copper from the north in trade, and this they hammered into sheets and cut to make bracelets and rings.

Copper played an important part in the Kwakiutl ceremonies, for the display of it represented wealth. For the potlatch ceremonies unique copper plaques were produced, some of which were painted black and engraved through the paint. Occasionally, in the excitement of the festivities, the chief would dramatically break the plaque into pieces as a challenge to the other chiefs to do likewise.

During the early days of settlement copper utensils were in great demand, particularly the large kettles, which were used by soapmakers, candlemakers, dyers and distillers. They were a necessity, and were snapped up despite the fact that they were very expensive. Those kettles were fine examples of craftsmanship. They were cut and hammered from sheet metal and were formed from one piece – of necessity, since copper can't be welded.

The coppersmiths also frequently made weathervanes for churches and homes, many of them three dimensional. The most popular design was the rooster, especially in Quebec where Chanteclair, the symbol of Peter's denial of Christ, served not only to tell the wind but to warn passersby about the evil of faithlessness.

"Tristan and Isolde," gold-plated copper goblet, by Andrew Goss, Toronto, Ontario

Pewter

Pewter, which is a silver-white alloy of various metals, including antimony, tin, lead and copper, has been widely used in everyday life for thousands of years. The Chinese were probably the first to make use of it, and continue to employ more of it than any other nation.

In the Western world, the Romans made extensive use of pewter for food containers, urns, cisterns, articles of various kinds. They added lead to make the metal more malleable, however, and there is a theory that the lassitude of the Romans before the fall of the Empire was due to lead poisoning from the extensive use of the alloy. Certainly the presence of lead can represent a threat, and the mediaeval trade guilds, as well as the French and British governments of the time severely restricted its use in pewter. So regulated, pewter continued to be popular for household wares up until the nineteenth century when it was finally displaced by cheap pottery, glass and woodenware. It was also the metal of the prosperous tradesman and artisan, who used it to imitate the silver displays of their customers and employers.

Pewter can be cut, bent, soldered or shaped by hammering. It can also be cast. Because it is soft, however, it cannot be used for knives, and is principally employed for pitchers and mugs. In the New World, where pewter soon took the place of woodenware for household utensils, it was generally cast. As it did not last long in daily use, many homes had their own moulds for remaking spoons. Itinerant pewter workers also melted and reworked the discarded pieces, using a "tinker's dam" – a cloth filled with damp sand – to keep the hot metal from flowing where it wasn't wanted.

Contemporary craftsmen are once again working with pewter. While some continue to make traditional tankards, candlesticks and porringers, others are experimenting with jewellery which becomes sculpture when not worn. The technique of pewter work has changed, too; the metal is now sometimes cast in rubber moulds or spun – an operation which is comparable to a potter using his wheel. And since Canadian-made pewter is now lead-free, food containers and platters of all kinds are made.

TOOLS OF THE SILVERSMITH

Silver

Silver, which has been alloyed with varying amounts of copper since the seventh century, to give it hardness and improve its working properties, has been used for jewellery, coinage, furnishings and bookcovers. It has even been used for pots and pans, since it is a good conductor of heat.

Until the mid-eighteenth century silver was used by the prosperous for cups, bowls and plates instead of the rarer glass and porcelain. It was also a standard of exchange that had a steady value, and was a sound investment when interest was sinful usury and when banks played a different role. When money was debased, turning the family wealth into useful objects was a safety measure. In prosperous times the collection was displayed prominently; in times of need it was melted. Some monarchs – Louis XIV and Charles I, for example – sacrificed their own silverware and that of their subjects to fill the treasury in national emergencies.

Naturally the silversmith, who could convert the silver from useful articles to money and back again, was an important man in the social scheme. And his role was further strengthened by the fact that according to canon law sacred vessels had to be made of silver or gold – which meant that as the Church increased in power and wealth, the silversmiths followed suit.

The English tradition of silverwork, which reached its height in the late seventeenth and early eighteenth century was carried to North America by the settlers. They brought some of their family plate with them and these pieces were frequently reworked. When this supply of metal ran out they melted silver dollars – the universal trade coin. So silversmithing, which had already taken firm root under the French regime, continued to flourish in Canada.

Silver craftsmen who moved to the Maritimes from the American colonies added their skills and versatility to the scene. And the patronage of the Church, the military and the trader barons gave great impetus to the craft.

At first the silver designs in French Canada were those inherited from the motherland. But as time went on the silversmiths of New France developed designs that were distinctively their own – still French in feeling but freed from rigid court standards. As a result, though their silver lost in magnificence, it gained in boldness. After the conquest

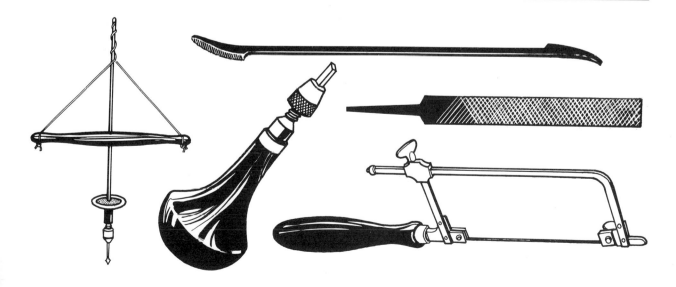

81

Silver and enamel wine goblets by A. Alan Perkins, Toronto, Ontario

the French artisans were isolated, thrown back on their own resources, and it was then that they began to produce their finest work, long after silversmithing in France had passed its peak. The work they did for the Church in Quebec at that time has no counterpart in the rest of Canada.

There was also an active production of silver for secular purposes in Quebec. When Montreal became the centre for the fur trade it also became the centre for silversmithing, and vast quantities of ornaments and articles were made for the Indian trade. The work was based on patterns and designs familiar to the Scottish merchants, and all of it was handmade. This lasted until the mid-nineteenth century when the introduction of gas permitted the use of the new Bunsen burner which gave a more intense heat than the earlier spirit lamps. Then the craft became more of a commercial operation and the craftsmen working by hand were forced out of business.

By the time silver trade articles were being made in Montreal, the Indians were working the metal themselves, though prior to the arrival of Europeans they had known it only in its natural state. But the early traders had introduced them to silver coins and ornaments and they had been greatly impressed by them. Queen Anne had made a good choice, then, when she had sent the chiefs of the Mohawks a beautifully made silver communion service, as a mark of her favour and esteem.

In Eastern Canada the silver articles made by the French and English for exchange in the fur trade were much sought after. They served to attract the allegiance of Indian allies at a time when European powers were struggling to establish a foothold in the New World.

The Indians were anxious to make their own silver articles, however, and were apparently making rapid headway in the art, since skilfully made Indian silver articles have been found at archeological sites – notably at Campbellford, Ontario. Thus when the fur trade declined, around 1800, the Indians were able to make their own trinkets, particularly brooches and gorgets. At first they copied the patterns of the trade pieces but in time they developed their own designs. And as the craft moved west from the Iroquois country to the plains and into the southwest of the United States, the designs were adapted to suit the tastes of the various tribes. Crowns, hearts and Masonic symbols were adapted. The Scottish double heart appeared so frequently that it came to be known as the Iroquois national emblem. The heart with a crown, called by the Indians Guardian of the Night, was also very popular.

*Gold and sterling necklace by William Reid, Montreal, Quebec**

About fifty years later the Indians on the west coast, who had been introduced to silver jewellery by the Russian traders in Alaska, also began to make their own ornaments for ceremonial use. They pounded coins into rings, bracelets and other articles, and incised them with conventionalized animal designs. They were superb craftsmen and created pieces that were genuine works of art. These served as status symbols, evidence of wealth and rank.

Today craftsmen working with silver are producing articles which bear little resemblance to traditional work. They are combining the silver with other metals and are experimenting with techniques and finishes. The designs, too, are innovative. Necklaces, for example, are now frequently made without clasps, and depend on the tensile quality of the metal itself to stay in position.

Gold

Gold is the most malleable of metals. It also will take on different colours, textures and finishes. It is no wonder, therefore, that though it is extensively employed in industry, its principal use is for jewellery and that it is the most sought-after of all metals for this purpose.

Goldsmithing dates from the Etruscan, Minoan, Assyrian and Egyptian civilizations but it was also produced and worked in India, Asia and South America at an early date. The Spanish conquest of Mexico in the sixteenth century resulted in a large increase of world gold reserves and gave great impetus to the craft.

Gold was discovered in Nova Scotia in 1849 but it wasn't until 1860 that prospectors showed much interest in the metal. Then the word was out and a number of European goldsmiths and jewellers emigrated to Canada to take advantage of the find. They also made use of the semiprecious stones that were available in abundance in the area. And so a new Canadian craft was begun. It was a losing battle for the hand-craftsmen, however, since they were faced with strong competition from gold manufacturers who employed a number of workers and used the latest machinery. It is only of recent years that the crafting of gold as an art has been revived.

Today the designer-artisans are less in awe of the metal than their predecessors, and are daring to produce articles that are modern in feeling and unusual in technique. They are also combining it with other metals and are using it as the setting for native or semiprecious stones rather than for gem stones.

Platinum Metals

The platinum metals, which include palladium and rhodium, were probably used in the ancient world, although the first mention of them appeared in European literature in the sixteenth century. Platinum as a pure substance was not used to any extent until the early nineteenth century, since it was only then that metallurgists learned how to separate it from the metals usually found with it.

Because metals in this group resist water, air and most acids, they are referred to as the "noble" metals, and are used by craftsmen in jewellery and for purely decorative objects, sometimes in conjunction with or alloyed with, gold. They are difficult to craft, however, and little work is being done with them at the present time.

Aluminum

Although aluminum is one of the most abundant metals in the earth's crust, it occurs in nature only in combined form, and was not isolated until the early nineteenth century. By the 1860's it was being produced commercially in small quantities, and by the 1880's it was being produced for household and industrial equipment. It was therefore considered primarily a commercial substance; it is only in the last decade or so that craftsmen have worked it by hand.

Aluminum is a malleable metal; it can readily be turned out in the form of sheets or wire. It is a good conductor of heat, is lightweight and non-corrosive. It is therefore admirably suited for both craft and commercial purposes.

The craftsmen currently working with aluminum are striving to free themselves from the traditional utilitarian forms associated with this metal. They are producing aluminum sculpture and decorative objects of all kinds.

Plastics

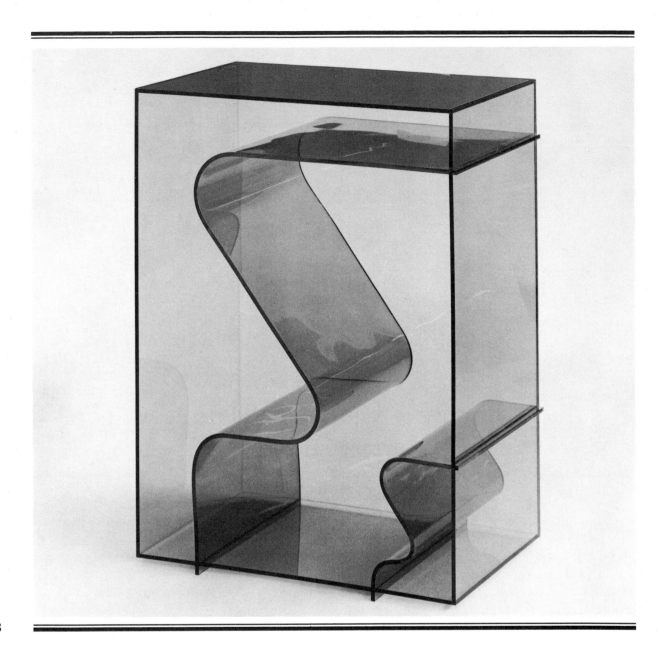

Plastic three-height table designed by Stephen Hogbin, Mississauga, Ontario

The term "plastic" is so familiar to us today that we tend to use it in the singular, as if all plastics were the same material. In reality, the only thing they have in common is the fact that they are versatile substances produced by combining carbon with oxygen, hydrogen, nitrogen and other elements – by-products of the petroleum industry. In other respects they possess quite different properties. The common name, "plastic," (from the Greek, meaning "capable of being formed") is applicable only because they share one fundamental characteristic – they can all be readily moulded.

Thermosplastics, one of the two basic types, while hard and rigid at normal temperatures, become soft and mouldable or malleable when heated. When soft, this type of plastic can be given shape, and the shape will be retained when the material cools. Even when reheated and remoulded, it will return to the original shape each time. This may be done a number of times before the plastic deteriorates, which gives the craftsman the opportunity to alter the design or correct mistakes.

Thermosetting plastics, which possess quite different properties, can be shaped only once, since heating them causes a chemical change in which the molecules become tightly interlinked. Once the plastic becomes rigid it will never return to its original state.

Some plastics can be shaped by hand; others have to be moulded, put under pressure, or treated by a combination of these methods. They can also be woven, twisted, cut and sawn. They may be ground, sewn, folded, engraved, etched, embossed, printed and airblasted! They can be combined with textile fibres, weeds, grains, pebbles, gems or metals.

In the last twenty years plastics have taken over the role of many ancient and traditional materials – wood, glass, metal, clay and wool – and have invaded crafts from furniture-making to weaving. The textile crafts are particularly dependent on plastics, since polyesters are now considered essential materials for weaving, knitting, crocheting and stitchery.

Much remains to be learned about working with plastics as a distinctive discipline, however. Plastics are too often used to imitate traditional materials; they should be employed for their own characteristics – their ability to refract light and retain colour, their malleability, and other attributes. Their potential as craft material has not yet been fully explored and the medium presents a great challenge to the artisan-designers who are opening an entirely new field.

Plastic furniture, jewellery, boxes and other craft objects are now being made and instruction in the art is being offered at some colleges. It is to be hoped, then, that soon there will be a number of plastic workers who will be able to shake off the restrictions of traditional crafts and bring out the special qualities of this contemporary material. As Peter Drucker said in *The Age of Discontinuity*, "Plastics is the only major industry rooted in twentieth century rather than in nineteenth century science – and is only a faint premonition of what the 'materials' industry of tomorrow will likely be."

Rug-making

The earliest form of floor coverings were rushes, which were interwoven or trampled and felted into a mass. At a very early period, however, animal fibres were being spun and woven to make rugs. Fragments of this kind of fabric, found near the Caspian Sea, have been dated by radiocarbon tests as having been made around 6000 B.C.

It is not known exactly when the first pile rugs were made, but pieces of linen with pile threads looped at right angles to the backing have been found in Egyptian tombs of the XI Dynasty which flourished around 2000 B.C. Our Turkish towels and hooked rugs are descendents of this type of construction.

Wool carpets with pile knotted into the warp were also made in the Eastern world long before the Christian era. Turkey and Persia seem to have been preeminent in the field even then, since the two varieties of knots used were called Ghiordes and Sehna after towns in those countries. Rugs of this type were also made in China, India, Turkestan and Caucasia, and came to be known as Oriental rugs.

An interesting addition to the incomplete jigsaw of rug history was made in 1953 when a Russian archeologist found burial mounds in southern Siberia which he dated at 500 B.C. Beneath the cairns and perfectly preserved in the permafrost, were burial furniture, clothing, chariots – and a carpet that had been used as a saddle cloth. The carpet was an excellent example of Turkish knotting but the design was of Persian origin, which would indicate that nomadic tribes spread the art of carpet weaving throughout Asia.

The first carpet factories were set up in Istanbul by the Turks who for centuries dominated the Near East. They mainly used abstract or geometric patterns because the religion of the Moslems forbade them to make lifelike images of living things. Eventually the Moors carried the tradition into Spain, and soon the Spaniards too had set up factories and were producing rugs of Moorish design.

After the expulsion of the Moors, the Catholic Church forbade the use of Islamic designs in the decorative arts, and Spanish rug-weavers had to create new patterns. The industry continued to prosper, however, and it was not until the late nineteenth century that the demand began to dwindle and the workmanship to decline.

The French imported Oriental rugs in great quantity until the sixteenth century when Henry of Navarre set up rug workshops to revive the country's economy after the devastating religious wars. As soon as the shops were in operation imports were forbidden. Consequently the leading designer-craftsman, Pierre Dupont, favoured by

Hooked tapestry by Yvonne Coallier, Montreal, Quebec

royal patronage, was extremely successful. Eventually he set up a large workshop in an old soap factory and produced carpets which came to be known as Savonneries, from the soap association. In the eighteenth century the French craftsmen extended their tapestry technique to the making of rugs without pile, producing beautiful Aubusson carpets which, though not as durable as Savonneries, are still unsurpassed for design, colour and workmanship.

The English acquired a taste for Oriental rugs from the returning Crusaders and built up a home industry using Oriental motifs as well as designs based on their own native flowers and those illustrated in the great seventeenth-century herbal books. In time, English rugs also showed the influence of Indian and Chinese patterned textiles which traders brought back with them from the East, but the exotic designs were always expressed in English terms.

The industry in England received an infusion of new blood when Huguenot textile workers sought sanctuary there after the Edict of Nantes was revoked in 1685. The French carpet-weavers settled in Wilton in southern England, and to this day Wilton remains a rug manufacturing centre.

It was not only the Spanish, French and English who favoured Oriental rugs, however. Most European countries set up factories to produce their own versions of the highly-prized imports. But however skilful the imitators became they never succeeded in equalling the craftsmanship of the originators.

Perhaps that is because from very early times the people of the East had been making rugs in vast quantities, not only for export but for domestic use as well. And the demand for domestic use was tremendous. Every man had to have his own prayer rug, with an arrow or other point in the design to indicate which way it should be placed to face toward Mecca. Nomads had to have rugs, which they could roll up and transport easily, to take the place of chairs and beds. People in settled communities required rugs to cover walls, floors, beds and furniture. Rugs were, in effect, essential to the lifestyle of the Asiatics.

In such a case it is not surprising that a body of traditions developed around the industry. Each rug-making community had its own colourings and patterns which were handed down from generation to generation. The range of colours in each instance was not wide; while carpets might be of enormous size and intricately patterned, they were seldom worked with more than a dozen colours.

Many craftsmen use a punch needle for making rugs. They push the needle through the backing as far as it will go, catch the loop between their thumb and index finger, and hold it while they withdraw the needle, to plunge it in once more a little further along. One side of the needle is slotted, and this side must always be faced in the direction the work is proceeding.

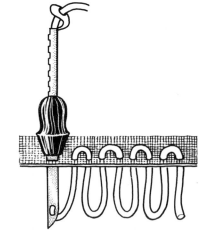

Rug, wool on canvas — punch technique, by Dzintra Baird, Toronto, Ontario. (Royal Trust Company, Toronto)

The patterns included symbols of religious significance. The swastika, the sun wheel and the tree of life appeared frequently. The tree of life, which was the symbol of paradise, always assumed the shape of a tree indigenous to the area in which the rug was woven. Sometimes it was a cyprus, sometimes a pine, sometimes a palm. In Persia and India abstract floral designs were common, and scrollwork and medallions were widely used. In Turkey and Spain geometric designs predominated. In China dragons, the phoenix, peonies and chrysanthemums were favourite motifs.

In the early days rugs were woven on primitive portable looms and the yarns were dyed with plants and vegetables. Dyeing was the work of the old women who kept their recipes secret and passed them along only to their daughters. The weaving and knotting was done by the young women and children who had supple fingers and small hands. Sometimes there were several hundred knots to the square inch.

Several weavers would sit at one loom, working out the design according to the instructions of a caller who chanted the colours. The callers were highly regarded professionals. They could remember hundreds of patterns and were able to dictate from right to left or vice versa at will. No rug was ever completely perfect, however. Perfection was regarded as an attribute of God alone, and some small error was always made, deliberately, as an acknowledgement of this fact.

The intricate designs of these early rugs required very painstaking, delicate work. And when the Persian culture began to decline in the eighteenth century the standards of workmanship also began to slip. Eventually this type of weaving was practically abandoned, and though it was revived in the 1870's – on a much coarser scale – the hand-made Oriental rugs of today are much inferior to those made prior to the eighteenth century.

The Oriental rug was not the only type being made in Europe from the time of the Middle Ages. The Scandinavians had adopted the Rya knitting technique which was known to the Egyptians and the Vikings, and which was later practised in many parts of Europe.

Originally, the Rya method was employed to produce shaggy, warm textiles which were used for bedcovers, sleigh or boat rugs, saddle blankets, or as draught-checks for doorways. Later it was used mainly to make rugs which took their name from their technique.

96

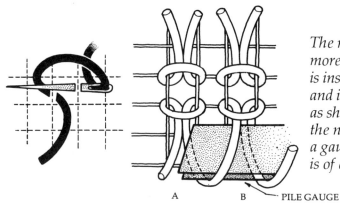

A   B   PILE GAUGE

The rya or Ghiordes knot is tied around two or more warp ends. The needle, threaded with yarn, is inserted behind one warp, then carried back and inserted behind the warp to the right of it, as shown in A. The craftsman then moves on to the next knot, carrying the yarn under and over a gauge, as shown in B, to ensure that the pile is of even length, if that is thought desirable.

In the early days Ryas were woven in tones of black, grey and white, without pattern. Later weavers worked in stripes, used religious symbols, and sometimes added armourial bearings. Today Ryas are made in lively colours and are generally designed as hangings rather than as floor coverings.

A similar rug is the Flossa, which originated in Finland – also as a textile. It differs from the Rya in that it has a very short pile and a greater tufting density. Both of these rugs were forerunners of the modern, commercially produced shag.

The Europeans who came to North America left a world where rugs were in fairly common use. They entered one in which floor coverings of any kind were a luxury that could be afforded by few. The wealthy imported rugs, those connected with the fur trade used pelts, but most settlers' homes had cold floors of tamped earth or planked wood. As soon as they could spare the time, therefore, the pioneers hooked, braided or wove rugs, using precious scraps of cloth which they salvaged from worn-out bedding and clothes.

When professional weavers appeared on the scene the making of rugs constituted an important part of their trade. The most popular product of their looms was a brightly striped wool carpet similar to the drugget manufactured in England. It was generally made from wool rags supplied by the housewife who cut them into strips, sewed them together, and then wound them into a ball. The carpet was woven in narrow widths and the strips were sewn together to make a rug or cover a room completely.

In her book *Canadian Settler's Guide* published in 1857, Catharine Parr Traill describes the process of preparing the rags for the weaver:

"A pound and a half of rags will make one yard of carpet, with the warp. Many persons dye the warp themselves: lie of wood-ashes, with a little copperas makes a deep yellow: logwood and copperas makes a black, and indigo and lee [lye] from the house, gives a full blue. Made up with the coloured warp, the carpet looks better, and does not dirty so soon.

"The white cotton rags are better washed clean, and then dyed with any of these dyes. Those who do not care to take this trouble, use them as they are, but they soil soon.

"The best sort of rag-carpet is made by intermitting the colours as much as possible, cutting the strips through, instead of turning the corners: you have more work in joining, but the effect is better; and there are no unsightly ends on the surface of the carpet. Bits of bright red flannel, of blue, green, or pink mousselin-de-laine, or stuffs of any bright colour, old shawls and handkerchiefs, and greene baize, will give you a good,

Precut yarn is used in hooking rugs with a latch hook. It is therefore possible to change colour frequently. As the drawings show, the yarn is looped around the shaft of the hook, the hook is pushed through into the next hole, and the yarn ends are caught in the hook. A tug closes the latch and the yarn ends are pulled through the loop to make a knot which is then tightened.

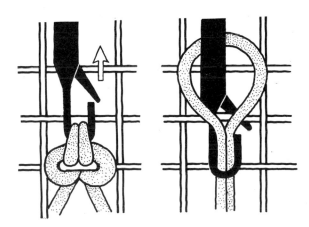

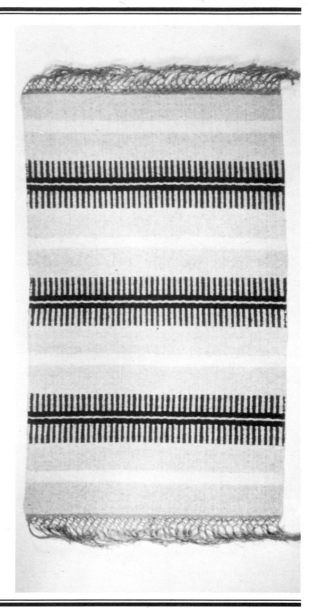

Contemporary Salish rug. Hat in foreground is woven spruce root (Nootka), also contemporary. (Canadian Guild of Crafts, Quebec)

Rug by Maurice Clayton, Ottawa, Ontario

long-enduring fabric that will last for eight or ten years, with care. Children can be taught to cut the rags, and join and wind into balls, ready for the weaving."

Very few of these carpets are in existence today, for rag carpeting became associated in the minds of the pioneers with poverty, and as soon as possible families purchased imitation Oriental rugs from mail-order houses. The craft gradually died out, and today hand-woven rugs of the pioneer type are seldom made except in rural Quebec and in the Acadian settlements of the Maritimes.

The tradition of hand-making rugs continues in the hooking process, however. With a short-handled hook similar to a crochet hook the wool is pulled in loops through a foundation fabric. It is an ancient craft that apparently began in Scandinavia, was taken to England, and brought to the east coast of North America by seamen who had been hooking rugs for a long time. It has flourished in North America ever since, particularly in the Maritimes.

The hooking of rugs was done in the home after the chores were done. But in the winter months women held hooking bees at which they exchanged gossip and patterns, and swapped yarn.

In the early days hooked rugs were made of strips cut from discarded garments, grain and feed bags looped into a backing of linen, canvas or grain-bag jute. For designs some women took their inspiration from what they saw around them: houses, barns, farm animals, dogs and cats. Some copied patterns from the imported chinaware and wallpaper, and some made stencils from cups and saucers, or drew around leaves and fern fronds.

Braided rugs were also popular during pioneer days. They too could be made of rag-bag pieces of cloth, and either cotton or wool would serve – though wool was preferred as it was easier to keep clean. The rags were washed, cut into strips, joined, braided, and finally sewn together in coiled strips. Colouring was done in a hit-and-miss way, but an accomplished rug-maker would make an effort to balance the bright with the dark. The rug was added to from time to time as more material came to hand; in fact, it sometimes grew while it was in use.

Braided rugs are still being made but the present-day craftsmen-designers seem to find more excitement in hooking, tufting and weaving than in braiding rugs.

In general, contemporary rug-making breaks all the traditional rules and techniques.

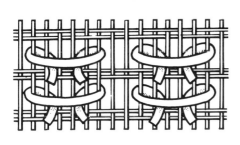
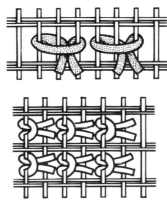
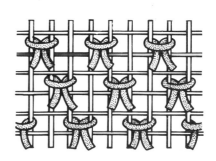

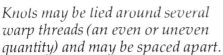
Knots may be tied around several warp threads (an even or uneven quantity) and may be spaced apart.

They may also be staggered, or they may be formed sideways. The spacing depends on yarn thickness.

"Twilight of the Gods," tapestry by Friedel, Peterborough, Ontario

Rya rug by Gertrude Michel, Richmond Hill, Ontario

The materials are no longer the conventional silk, cotton and wool; leather, plastic, reed, fur, twine and jute, and a great many other substances are equally favoured. Techniques also have changed; now embroidery, crochet knitting and fringing are all employed to vary the texture and pattern. And the emphasis today is on originality, colour, texture, and on the total creative effect, rather than on detailed workmanship.

In one respect, however, the hand-made rugs have gone full cycle. As in the past, many of them are now hung on the wall or used as bed throws rather than simply as floor coverings.

Stitching

Embroidery

The term "embroidery" is used to describe the embellishment of fabrics with decoration produced by hand or machine stitching. It includes needlepoint, petit point and crewel work, but it does not include tapestry, because true tapestry is woven.

There are twelve basic embroidery stitches which have come down to us from ancient times. From combinations of these, needleworkers have produced magnificent works of art, including the famous Bayeux Tapestry, which is not really a tapestry at all but an embroidered depiction of the Norman Conquest in 1066, worked out in cartoon-strip fashion along a 230-foot length of linen.

Though embroidery was practised by the Egyptian, Greek and Roman women, many historians believe it achieved its greatest refinement in England during the great period of church ornamentation that took place during the twelfth to fourteenth centuries. Certainly the craft was carefully cultivated in that country; at a very early age small girls spent long hours practising the traditional embroidery stitches, and the making of samplers was considered an important part of their education.

Embroidery continued to flourish during the period when gentlewomen had time on their hands. Mary Queen of Scots, a famous needlewoman, whiled away her long imprisonment by embroidering exquisite wall and bed hangings and working souvenirs for her attendants.

Although the British made embroidery their special art, it was practised throughout the world, and each country contributed a special touch. The Persians introduced embroidered family crests to household furnishings; the French were adept at backstitch, and the Ukrainians and Scandinavians developed intricate cross-stitch patterns.

Traditional embroidery pieces included samplers, coverlets, bed curtains, clothing and church vestments and hangings. Heavier pieces, including chair covers, fire screens, hangings, and even rugs, were usually done on canvas and covered the background material completely. Some of the earliest surviving pieces of canvas embroidery were worked in satin and cross stitches which are the easiest to do. But generally canvas stitchery consists of straight stitches placed side by side or overlapped for texture. Counting threads lessens the guess-work, and the art of canvas work – or needlepoint, as it is sometimes called – is to change size and direction of the stitch. This gives light, shade and texture.

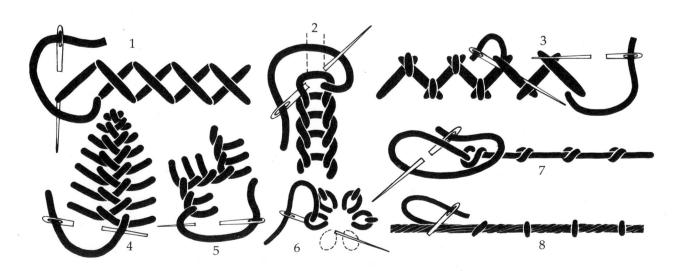

During the seventeenth century needlepoint was worked with about forty threads to the inch. This made a fine, flexible fabric even when the pattern was outlined by metal thread which not only gave richness but actually lengthened the life of the embroidery because it acted as a guard and prevented the silk from rubbing. At this time the background material was linen, and the technique included counted as well as free designs. Table covers, cushions and book covers were done in this manner, and some very fine pieces were produced.

Up until the mid-nineteenth century embroidery patterns were designed by the needleworker and were worked out in the colours and stitches of her choice. She occasionally received inspiration from fashion magazines, and she often passed on the tedious background stitching to her daughters, ladies-in-waiting, and upper servants; but the creation remained essentially her own. All this changed during the Victorian era, however. The growth of industrialization and the increase in the number of women's magazines made it possible for those who had never been taught the fine art of embroidery to cover stamped canvas or pierced paper with brightly coloured wool. This method was called Berlin work, and the fad for it swept Europe and North America. Kits that included canvas, shaded wool and directional charts were sold by mail. Embroidery was reduced to mechanical hand-work.

The colours used in Berlin work were garish and the designs were humdrum. Realistic embroidered pictures were very popular, and household pets, country scenes and bouquets were favourite subjects. Women who could not master pictorial subjects were content to embroider on canvas or paper such bromides as God Bless Our Home; Faith, Hope and Charity; and Be Good. The passion for Berlin work became so intense that all other types of needlework went into a decline and some forms of stitchery practically disappeared.

The revival of embroidery as a creative craft can be attributed to William Morris who included needlework among his many interests. In order to rediscover forgotten stitches, he unpicked early embroideries to see how they were worked. Later he set up workshops and undertook commissions, employing skilled needleworkers. His embroidery was done on linen, mainly in wool but with the addition of some silk and metal threads. The designs were based on coiling stems, flowers and buds. It was Morris' influence that brought about the formation of the Royal School of Needlework in 1872 which trained

Some basic embroidery stitches: 1. Cross stitch, 2. Chain stitch, 3. Herringbone stitch couched down with small stitches, 4. Cretan or feather stitch, 5. Double-feather stitch, 6. Lazy-daisy stitch, 7 & 8. Couching stitches, 9. Diagonal satin stitch, 10. Variation of the buttonhole stitch, 11. French knot, 12. Bullion stitch (a long French knot). With these in her repertoire a needleworker can produce a great variety of embroidery patterns, from simple to intricate.

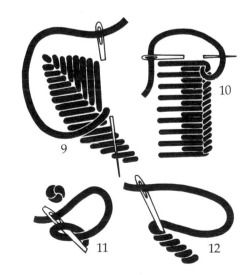

embroiderers and influenced taste for many years.

It is interesting to note that while embroidery has traditionally been the province of women, in the late nineteenth century needlework pieces were being designed and created by men. Burne-Jones and Walter Crane as well as William Morris publicly exhibited their work.

By the end of the century the *Art Nouveau* movement was in full flower and embroidery was one of its outstanding manifestations. The protagonists of the movement strongly opposed the popular conception that embroidery should imitate nature. They believed that the design should come from the technique itself. In fact, when embroidering figures they emphasized the form with line rather than shading, and they did everything possible to avoid the realism of flesh tones.

In Canada the Indians had their own styles of embroidery. Over the centuries they had learned to work with birchbark as if it were the most supple cloth, to knit corn husks as if they were silken ribbons, and to use the sweet grasses, turtle shells and other natural substances in very effective ways. They based their pattern on geometric talisman figures as well as on flowers and animals, and though the white men – particularly the French – had an influence on their designs, many of their indigenous symbols are still basic to their work.

The Indians were especially skilled in embroidering with porcupine quills – a craft unique to North America. In 1809 Alexander Henry, the fur trader, wrote, "They appear to great advantage, having their cap, shirt, leggings and shoes perfectly clean and white, trimmed with porcupine quills and other ingenious work of their women."

Porcupine quills are smooth and shiny, but become flexible when soaked in water, and are easy to dye. Dyed and dried, they are sewn or poked into skin, cloth or bark. This type of embroidery was used to decorate moccasins, shirts and leggings, as well as birchbark boxes which were made to trade with the white settlers. Every tribe had its own style of box and embroidery. For example, the Ottawas made round baskets to hold sewing utensils, and decorated them with naturalistic animals, while the Micmacs made their boxes with vaulted tops.

Woven quillwork was also common among the Indians of central Canada. Nicolas Denys, an Acadian settler and fur-trader, described the craft in his book *Description géographique et historique des costes de l'Amerique septentrionale*, published in 1672: ". . . the

Chairback made by the Micmac Indians at Shubenacadie, Nova Scotia about 1890 (Nova Scotia Museum Collection)

"Dressing Room," fabric collage wall hanging by Diana Bennett Orris, Toronto, Ontario

"Bandera," stitchery fabric collage by Carole Sabiston, Victoria, British Columbia

belles, who wish to appear pretty, and who know how to do good work, make ornamental pieces of the size of a foot or eight inches square, all embroidered with Porcupine quills of all colours. It is made on a frame, of which the warp is threads of leather from unborn Moose, a very delicate sort; the quills of Porcupine form the woof which they pass through the threads, just as one makes tapestry, and it is very well made. All around they make a fringe of the same threads, which are also encircled with these Porcupine quills in a medley of colours."

Another type of embroidery at which the Indians were particularly skilled was hair embroidery, which was used to decorate clothing, belts, pouches and moccasins. Moose or elk hair was used, either in its natural colour or dyed. It was then sewn to garments with fibres. This type of work is very difficult, because the hair, being very short and slippery, is hard to manipulate. So though the Indians were very adept at the art their designs were usually very simple. When the French Ursuline nuns set up schools for French and Indian girls, however, they taught their pupils to embroider in the European tradition, using the hair as if it were silk. It was excruciatingly tedious work. The hair had to be wet to give it pliability. The needle had to be punched through the cloth before it was threaded, and it had to be rethreaded for almost every stitch.

At first this type of embroidery was used for altar cloths and vestments. Later secular articles such as card cases, spectacle containers and pincushions were made. The pincushions, which were made of bark, were particularly popular among the government and military families who returned to Europe from Canada. In the 1830's such pieces were known as "Indian curios," and it is possible that the craft influenced European women who at this time began to embroider and crochet using human and horse hair.

Bead work was also developed to a high art by the Indians. Before the coming of the Europeans the beads were generally made of seeds or shells, and they were worked with elk hair on leather in designs that varied from tribe to tribe. After the advent of the white man glass beads were used, and they were usually stitched to cloth, but the patterns, for the most part, remained distinctively Indian.

Beads were used to decorate moccasins, ceremonial clothing, pouches and blankets. Belts of wampum beads made from the shells of clams were particularly highly prized. They were exchanged at treaty signings and on special occasions were given as gifts.

Because of the roughness of pioneer living, few women in early Canada had the opportunity to continue the embroidery they had learned in their homelands. When life became more gentle, however, those who weren't influenced by the great variety of kits offered by peddlers, magazines and newspapers took up the traditional work they had learned as children. The Ukrainians and people from Iceland, Sweden and France embroidered linens, shirts and dresses, using the same patterns they had been taught.

In recent years embroidery has undergone a startling transformation. Today's needleworker is less concerned with producing a painstakingly perfect piece of work than with expressing a personal concept through the use of a wide range of materials and techniques.

To achieve a desired effect appliqué and collage may be combined with decorative stitching done by hand or machine. Padding may be used to produce relief designs in which light and shadow serve as part of the medium, or even to produce three dimensional objects.

Today's embroidery backing is just as likely to be leather or paper or plastic as it is to be canvas or textile, and the traditional wool, silk or cotton embroidery yarn may be raffia, string or any other pliable substance.

Contemporary embroidery is sophisticated, disciplined, yet highly imaginative. Where once the addition of buttons or sequins or dried weeds would have been frowned upon, the incorporation of such materials is now taken for granted if they are to suit the designer's purpose.

In keeping with this attitude and contrary to the traditional belief that anything made mechanically cannot be as fine or as sensitive as a handmade article, there is a growing use of the sewing machine for embroidery. While there is a danger that the sewing machine might lead to stereotyping, in the hands of a skilled craftsman-designer it is a tool in the same way as a potter's wheel is a tool. The final results are controlled by the worker's skill and taste.

The modern sewing machine makes possible the creation of new textures. Stitches can be applied layer upon layer to achieve a sculpture effect almost impossible to duplicate by hand. It is possible for the craftsman to vary tensions, select embroidery stitches, and switch from one coloured thread to another (or, indeed, to combine various colours) with the flick of a finger. The sewer is now able to use not only thread but rug yarn, plastic strips, and even fine metal wire.

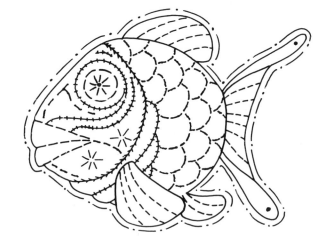

It was customary for children in Victorian days to work a sampler which included the various embroidery stitches. The fish demonstrates:

OUTLINE STITCH	————	
STRAIGHT STITCH		
SEQUIN		
BACKSTITCH	— — —	
COUCHING	+++++++++	
THORN STITCH	⟩⟩⟩⟩⟩	

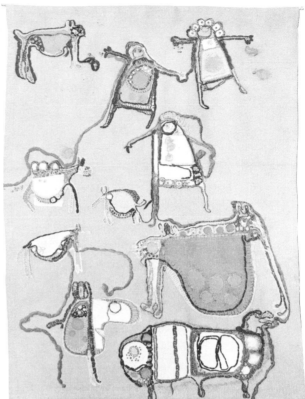

"Sea of Neutrality," fabric collage and embroidery by Carole Sabiston, Victoria, British Columbia*

Embroidery by Wendy Toogood, Calgary, Alberta

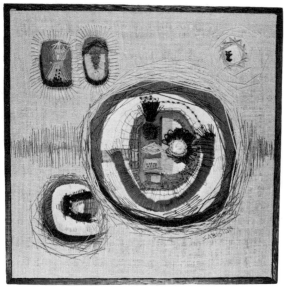

*Mukluks by Mrs. Ernest Jebb, LePas, Manitoba**

"Commerce," banner in wools by Mary Vaitiekunas, Vancouver, British Columbia

"Inscape," embroidery and fabric collage by Carole Sabiston, Victoria, British Columbia

"Don Quixote," fabric collage hanging by David and Susan Klahr, Toronto, Ontario

The use of the sewing machine has also revived and extended the possibilities inherent in ancient drawn-thread work – the technique whereby threads are drawn to form open-work patterns and the resulting holes secured by stitchery or tied together in groups. Traditionally, drawn-thread work was used for clothing and household furnishings, but after the mid-nineteenth century when this type of embroidery reached its zenith, it degenerated into fussiness. The sewing machine has brought new freshness, spontaneity and strength to the work. It allows the embroiderer to pull threads and hold them in position while reinforcing is done. It also makes it possible for the competent craftsman to incorporate darning stitches which add both strength and texture to open-work designs. As a result, it is now practical to make large pieces that can hang free as sculpture or be utilized as a form of lace fabric.

It is clear, then, that the sewing machine has opened up a new avenue of creative needlework. It is not as concerned with precision stitching and therefore leaves the craftsman freer to concentrate on design.

Appliqué & Fabric Collage

Appliqué, as the name implies, is the art of applying one piece of material to another. The top piece is cut out in design shape, the edges are tucked in, and the piece is sewn to a backing.

It is generally conceded that appliqué probably evolved from the ancient chore of patching. At some point someone found the overlay effect attractive, and from that point on appliqué became an art – a simple and effective way of adding colour and pattern to fabrics.

It was not until the thirteenth century, however, when the Crusaders returned from the East bringing exotic needlework pieces of all kinds, that appliqué became popular in Europe. It was soon discovered that this form of stitchery was an effective way of displaying family crests on garments and banners.

Since then the use of appliqué has proliferated. It has been used for altar and lectern cloths, ecclesiastical vestments and banners, palls, pictures (particularly the "mourning pictures" popular in the eighteenth century), and for bed hangings and quilts.

The pioneer women in the New World were grateful for their skill in appliqué work. It enabled them to make use of small scraps of precious material to brighten up their homes. Printed fabrics were not available for some time after the first settlers arrived and for some time after that were highly taxed, so the small pieces salvaged from worn-out clothing were used to decorate the plain yard goods. This was particularly true of quilts that were made of whole cloth; those that were embellished with sewn-on flowers and foliage were highly prized and proudly displayed.

Even before the arrival of the settlers, however, some Indians and Eskimos were using appliqué to decorate their garments. It is not known whether this was an indigenous craft or whether the native people learned the art from contact with early explorers and traders. Whatever the source of their knowledge, they were very skilled, and to this day some fine work of this type is being done, particularly around Cape Dorset.

The Eskimo woman employs much the same appliqué technique as the European, applying skin patches in the shape of familiar objects – birds, fish, seals, and even the Eskimo crescent-shaped knife – to duffle-cloth or skin backing, and sewing them in place with fine stitches. Frequently she adds horizontal strips, for added strength as well as decoration.

Generally the Inuit worker visualizes her design in its entirety before she begins, and cuts the patterns without guidelines. Her compositions are bold and direct, a fact which makes the wall hangings she produces especially effective.

From this craft another Eskimo art form has evolved – that of the stencil print, which has become popular in the last twenty years. The skin out of which the appliqué patches have been cut is stretched until it is stiff, after which it can be used as a stencil for transferring designs to sealskin or paper. (It is rather interesting to note that while the women do the appliqué work, the men do the stencilling.)

The Indians also did appliqué work before the days of settlement, adorning their ceremonial robes and hunting jackets with good-luck talismans. A certain amount of this work is still done by the Indian people, but now the West Coast Indians have introduced a new note: they apply buttons to the backing, to supplement or create patterns.

A modern extension of the appliqué process is fabric collage which grew out of a late nineteenth-century art form. The word "collage" was coined from *papier côlé*, or "pasted paper," as used to describe a technique involving the application of wallpaper, newsprint, tickets, and other things to the surface of painted canvas, to add texture and dimension.

*Appliquéd wool wall hanging by Winnie Tatya Putumiraqtuq, Winnipeg, Manitoba**

"All the World's a Stage," felt appliqué quilted hanging by Marta Dal Farra, Toronto, Ontario

"Fish," fabric collage by Gwyneth Lennox, Stanstead, Quebec (Canadian Guild of Crafts, Quebec)

As adhesives improved, it became possible to use textiles instead of paper, and so to achieve heightened sculptural effects. This has evolved into contemporary fabric collage which now may include not only pasted applications but sewn ones as well. Such pieces are often embroidered, to give them emphasis, extra dimension and a pleasing tactile quality. The technique lends itself admirably to panels, hangings and banners, and at present some very innovative work of this type is being done.

Today textile hangings are enjoying revived popularity. Once again they are adding splashes of colour to austere walls, and they are frequently hung from the lofty ceilings over stairwells in public buildings.

The use of banners and hangings is a modern application of an ancient tradition. Bannners were used in the Near East from early days, to distinguish military divisions, and it is believed that the Romans adopted their custom of carrying rigid standards (generally made of leather) from that source. Cloth banners apparently did not appear until the time of the Roman conversion to Christianity under Constantine, but from that time they have been part of church regalia. They were particularly important during the Middle Ages because they constituted a quick and effective way to identify friend or foe. It was a useful function, since the full armour of the time, with its closed helmet, made it almost impossible to distinguish one person from another. The heraldic symbols which appeared on those mediaeval banners gradually became more and more elaborate, and even to this day symbols play an important part in the craft.

The impetus for non-military secular use of banners came from the craft and merchant guilds who used them to promote pride and loyalty in their members. This has carried over to the present, though contemporary craftsmen are taking a somewhat different tack. They are producing purely decorative banners and hangings that show the influence of the hard-edge graphic artists. They are also using supplementary techniques, such as silk-screening and fabric collage. The result, however, is basically the same. Modern banners are bold, direct, clearly visible from a distance, and are designed to be seen from below, preferably slightly moving in a gentle breeze.

Quilts

The word "quilt" came into English from the old French *cuilte,* which in turn derived from the Latin *culcitra* – a stuffed mattress or cushion. The term was applied not only to bed quilts which in the early days were thick and mattress-like, but also to the stitched and padded lining used under clothing or armour for warmth and protection.

It is believed that quilting originated a very long time ago in the East. The oldest known example of the work is a three-thousand-year-old appliquéd funeral pall which is now in the Cairo museum, but there are also in existence ancient pictures showing the Chinese wearing the quilted garments which are a traditional part of their winter garb.

As was the case with so many other crafts, quilting was brought to western Europe by the returning Crusaders who had adopted it for their armorial trappings and tunics. It was readily accepted in the West and came to be used for ecclesiastical garments and furnishings as well as for clothing and bedding.

From the very beginning there were two types of quilts – those with a pieced surface and those with a whole-cloth surface. The pieced, or patchwork, quilts were generally made of scraps of material sewn together. The whole-cloth quilts were made of either plain or printed material or textile that had been embroidered or appliquéd to add colour and interest. In either case the surface cloth was attached loosely to a layer of wadding and then tacked to a backing. The whole was then stitched through in lines or patterns, to make the article more durable and less bulky. To facilitate the sewing the quilt was usually stretched on a frame.

Craft historians are inclined to believe that quilting was introduced into North America by the English and Dutch who settled in the Thirteen Colonies. Apparently it was not customary to make quilts in New France; the furs that were in plentiful supply served well enough for bed throws. It was not until the United Empire Loyalists settled in the Maritimes, Eastern Townships and Upper Canada that bed coverings of this type were widely used in Canada.

By that time quilts had become part of the very fibre of the frontier way of life. They represented an ideal way to make practical use of the precious scraps of material that were so carefully hoarded. They supplied bright patches of colour in the dark log houses. And on cold winter nights they were warm yet lighter weight than pelts would have been.

"Firebird," stitchery banner by Mary
Vaitiekunas, Vancouver, British Columbia

Stitched felt on burlap by Andrea V. Smith,
Toronto, Ontario. (Froim and David Merkur)

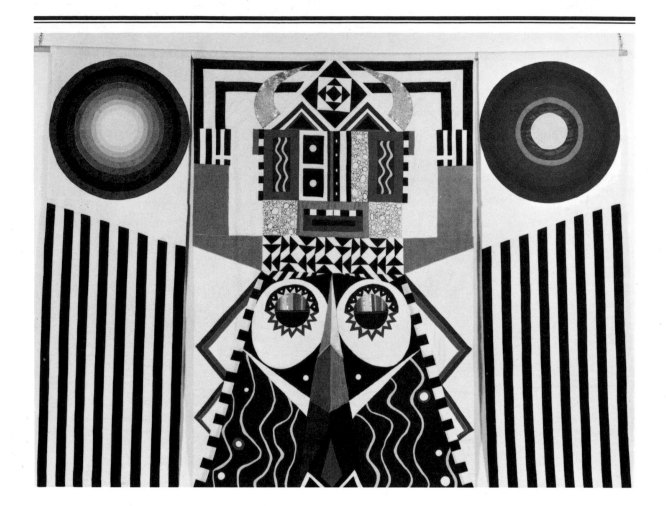

"Homage to Klee Wyck," appliquéd hanging by Eva Anna-Lisa Douglas, Thunder Bay, Ontario

Patterns like the Clam Shell, Log Cabin and Double Wedding Ring, (L to R), were once very popular for patchwork quilts, and cut-outs from printed textiles were often used for appliqué.

They could be washed and stored from one season to the next. They could be made in different thicknesses for the cold and not-so-cold weather. But, best of all, they were thrifty; even the padding and backing could be made from textiles so worn that they would not have withstood heavy use without reinforcement.

To the pioneer woman quilts represented more than usefulness, however. In many communities the quilting bees came to be the most important social functions of the season. Patterns and scraps were exchanged, along with gossip, and the workmanship of the other stitchers was examined critically. (Overlong stitches, called "toenail catchers," were regarded with great disfavour.)

Since only eight quilters could sit around a frame at one time, only the most skilful workers were invited to a bee. There was therefore much rivalry among those who sought the coveted places which would ensure them afternoons of companionship. Perhaps it was this aspect of the craft that caused it to linger on for many years after blankets and spreads were being factory produced.

Inevitably, customs and superstitions grew up around a craft that played such a large part in the social structure. Special quilts were made to mark special occasions: marriages, deaths, separations, coming-of-age. Of them all, however, the bridal quilt was regarded as the most important.

A bride's dower chest usually contained a baker's dozen of quilts – twelve for everyday use, the thirteenth for the bridal bed. They were usually pieced, they might even be embroidered, but they were never completed before a girl's betrothal; the wadding and backing were expensive and it was considered extravagant to do the actual quilting until marriage was assured. When an old trunk full of incomplete quilts is found today it is evidence of the fact that some young woman suffered from a broken heart or waited in vain for a husband.

There were other aspects to the bridal-quilt custom: While a girl might take part in many quilting bees, she never stitched her own bridal quilt. All she could do was make the first mark of the special pattern of stitches prescribed for that particular purpose. Love birds and hearts were considered suitable motifs and were reserved for trousseau linen; it was thought unlucky to use the heart shape in any other way.

The friendship quilting bee was the forerunner of the bridal shower. The making of this quilt involved two entertainments which were given by friends of the bride-to-be. At the

Quilt in The Blazing Star pattern hand-made in Nova Scotia for Suttles and Seawinds Limited. (All quilt photos Mark Gallant)

first party the blocks of coloured fabric were pieced together and at the second the top was quilted to the wadding and backing. It was obligatory for those who had given the pattern to do the stitching. Friendship quilts made of a series of squares autographed and embroidered were also given to pastors' wives leaving for a new congregation, or to women who were going West to settle.

The freedom quilt was the only one made for a man. In the late eighteenth and early nineteenth century becoming twenty-one was a major event. The young man no longer had to hand over his money to his parents; he no longer had to work at home for nothing. And to mark the occasion his girl friends would present him, on his birthday, with a freedom quilt. This was carefully laid away, along with his brand new tailor-made suit – quite possibly the only one he would possess during his lifetime – against the time when he would marry and lose his new-found freedom.

The memorial quilt was part of the social emphasis on mourning that took its impetus from Queen Victoria's excessive grieving. It was a patchwork made from the possessions, garments, even bookmarks and ties that had been owned by the deceased.

Quilting patterns evolved gradually as time and fabric became more generally available. The first quilted bed covers in Canada (made in the Maritimes) were merely large patches of linsey woolsey sewn together, padded with carded wool, and backed with homespun linen. They were warm, very thin, and quite dreary in appearance.

One of the next patterns to emerge was the crazy quilt, which was simply a melange of patches sewn together higgledy piggledy. The virtue of this type of cover was that any size or shape of scrap could be utilized, and if one patch wore out another could be added in its place. The crazy quilt gradually disappeared as textiles became less scarce, but was revived in the late 1870's – now an object of fashion rather than a symbol of thrift, now not relegated to the bedroom but proudly displayed in the parlour. No home of any pretention was complete without a crazy quilt thrown over a chair or a chaise longue

Of course the quilt patterns were given names, some of them quite amusing. There was the Double Monkey Wrench (also known as the Loveknot); there was the Duck's Foot, In-the-mud, Hold-the-barn-door, Puss-in-the-corner and Shoo-fly. And there was the Rose of Sharon, which derived its name from "The Song of Songs," the most passionate love lyric of all time. It was very popular for bridal quilts – at a time when women were generally supposed to be passive and shy of sex.

Other quilts were the Dresden Plate (also known as Aster), Friendship Ring, Pinetree, Log Cabin and Lemon Star (which was named after the Explorer Pierre LeMoyne!). Perhaps the best known – next to the Rose of Sharon – was the Star of Bethlehem.

Early quilts were made in various sizes, depending on locality. Some were huge, to cover the feather beds enjoyed by those of German ancestry. Others were small, to cover the trundle beds that were slipped under the four-posters during the daytime. Over the years quilt sizes became standardized, however. From the early nineteenth century most of them were made in a width that would fit our three-quarter beds. But they were short, according to our standards, and this was because the beds were short. It was customary to sleep in an almost upright position, reclining on several pillows.

Though at first quilts were made of household rag-bag scraps, as life became easier and quilting became a household craft, women began to buy cotton textiles for the purpose. The stores had a limited selection, however, and this is one of the reasons why collectors find quilts with the same textiles turning up repeatedly in a particular area.

The most usual textiles for quilts were wool, cotton and linen. Silk was rarely used, not only because it was very expensive and therefore rare in pioneer homes, but because its life was very short. It was occasionally used as an accent on an appliqué quilt, however, particularly if the coverlet was one of the picture type which show the life and adventures of the woman who sewed it. There are many charming quilts of this kind still in existence; they depict the birth of the maker, her courtship and marriage, her first log home, the first child, and – if she were fortunate – her second substantial home made of brick, clapboard or stone. Some even show the tragedies in her life.

Linen was generally used for backing a quilt, because of its durability. It wasn't considered suitable for the top, however, since it was seldom made in any colour other than natural beige.

Many pieced quilts were made of wool – either homespun or store-bought, and most of the material had seen previous service. In pioneer days when cooking was done over open fires, women generally wore woolen dresses even in the summer, because flying sparks would smoulder in wool, rather than flare as they did in cotton. The prevalence of wool in the family wardrobe was reflected in the quilts on their beds.

The simplest quilting consists of single lines of stitching running diagonally across the quilt – never parallel with the weave. This not only shows the pattern to better advantage,

Quilts hand-made in Nova Scotia in traditional patterns. On the left, Sunflower; on the right Kites and Spiderwebs.

but the cloth is less apt to tear or pull apart. In early quilts the lines were spaced about half an inch apart. In contemporary quilts they are wider apart – usually an inch and a half – because the filling is bulkier today.

Early quilts were hand stitched and the stitch patterns were very intricate. They included geometrics, feathers, flowers and shell patterns, the last of which was very common in coastal areas. The pattern was usually chalked on the backing and elaborate measures were taken to keep the markings even. Contemporary quilting is far less intricate and is frequently machine stitched.

The Loyalists who came from the southern part of the United States brought with them a type of quilting known as trapunto, in which only portions of the top design are padded. This type of spread is still popular in southern France and Italy where there is little need for the warmth of heavy covers.

Among the cottons, the most highly prized for quilt use were the prints. Printed materials were rare and very expensive, however, so thrifty women extended them by cutting the colourful patterns away from their background and appliquéing the pieces on to a plain ground of cotton or linen. All the parts of the print were used – birds, trees, flowers and people. Usually the figures were sewn on separately, but occasionally larger portions were applied as a zig-zag or a tree based on the Tree of Life patterns so popular in rugs, ceramics and chintzes in the eighteenth century. Sometimes, too, the women cut shapes out of colourful plain fabric and appliquéd them to the background.

The appliqué quilts were always reserved for guests and special occasions because, since they were more difficult to make than plain or pieced quilts, they were regarded as Sunday Best. And pioneer etiquette demanded that the spare bed be decked in the finest quilt to welcome a visitor – other than close kin, of course. If a visitor was shown to a bedroom in which there was an old quilt the meaning was well understood.

In the early days worn homespun blankets, carded sheep's wool, milkweed down and moss were used for padding, and sometimes sweet-smelling herbs were added. (In fact, women often made quilted pillows stuffed with soporific plants such as hops and catnip. These were at first used for invalids, but later became parlour accessories, and eventually commercial souvenirs.) When the cotton industry developed, cotton batting was used for wadding, but today wool and cotton batting have largely been replaced by polyester which is fluffier.

Huron Indian pouch made of dyed moosehair sewn on to a deerskin base. The orange fringe is dyed deer hair. (Museum of the American Indian)

At first quilting frames were homemade. Later they were sold by general stores and carpenters. In construction, the quilting frame was similar to a modern curtain stretcher. There were four strips of wood about an inch thick, two to four inches wide, and generally ten to twelve feet long. Along the edges of these strips, heavy ticking was tacked, and to this the quilt was pinned or basted. The four corners of the frame were fastened together by wooden pegs or iron clamps. The frames were adjustable; the wooden strips could be moved as the stitching progressed, and the quilt was rolled up.

Most frames were supported on the top of low-backed chairs of the same height. In some parts of the country, particularly in Quebec where there were deep window frames, one end would rest on the sill, the other on a kitchen chair or table.

As time went on frames became more elaborate, but the principle was always basically the same.

The great period for Canadian quilt-making was from the late eighteenth century to 1860 when the invention of the sewing machine and the mass production of textiles changed the social climate. The rapid industrialization of both Canada and the United States had a deadening effect on quilting, as it did on many home crafts. Women could then buy inexpensively what they once had had to save, and a great deal of the incentive to make quilts was lost.

At the same time quilts became the victims of changing taste. The third quarter of the nineteenth century was a period of ostentation, and machine-made articles were considered much more fashionable than humble home-made ones. Handcrafts stagnated.

The rebirth of crafts – particularly quilting – is probably due to the Philadelphia Centennial Exhibition in 1876. Strangely enough, while the exhibition celebrated the industrial growth of the United States, one of its most popular attractions was the eighteenth-century handwork. That display attracted a great deal of attention and created an incentive for the revival of stitchery.

But the rebirth was very difficult. This more affluent society had a taste for intricate work, and an intricate, hand-stitched quilt required time and endless patience. As a result the sewing machine was brought into play, and quilts were no longer made by hand in the larger centres.

In rural areas custom quilt-making has continued, largely through the efforts of

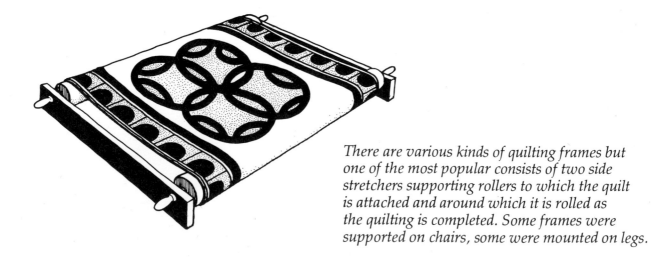

There are various kinds of quilting frames but one of the most popular consists of two side stretchers supporting rollers to which the quilt is attached and around which it is rolled as the quilting is completed. Some frames were supported on chairs, some were mounted on legs.

Contemporary quilts designed by Vicki Lynne Crowe, New Germany, Nova Scotia.
Bluenose II, The Star of Annapolis Royal.

women's organizations which take orders and organize quilting bees. Most such groups are still producing quilts in traditional patterns and many of them are still doing hand stitching, though there is a tendency now for sewing machines to be used for part of the operation.

The crafter of contemporary quilts is doing something quite different. She is producing quilts that are unique expressions of her creative imagination, working with new long-lasting, fade-proof textiles, and using a mixture of stitchery. The basis, of course, is still the three layers of cloth, but the decoration may include crochet, embroidery or bead-work.

Like many other craftsmen, the contemporary quilt designer is influenced by art training, and there is a definite relationship now between the quilt and op art. Many modern pieces are really soft sculpture. There is great emphasis on the tactile and the juxtaposition of matte and shiny textiles, which gives a very sensual appearance. Patterns run the gamut from the pictorial, which can include political slogans or poetry, to the pure abstracts.

Whether they are contemporary works of art or in the old bedcover tradition, however, quilts are still judged by the same standards. Fine, even stitching, pleasing colour schemes, balanced pattern, and careful finishing (including well-made corners and edging) are still the criteria of excellence.

Stone, Bone & Horn

The making of the first stone tools, which marked the beginning of the Stone Age, represented the most important turning point in man's development. The simple arrowheads which he then produced, by chipping one stone against another, meant that he was no longer the hunted but the hunter.

The oldest known domestic utensil was a hand mill which was used to crush grain. In design it was almost identical to mills used in many societies ever since, from the time of the Pharoahs to pioneer days in Canada. Its appearance heralded the production of a vast quantity of utilitarian articles, including knives, benches, ovens, cooking pots and lamps. And when the Babylonians and Assyrians invented the drill and other tools for working stone, craftsmen were able to achieve a balance and finish beyond the demands of functional use.

Though people of many ancient civilizations were extremely skilled in their stonework, the Egyptians were probably the most accomplished. Their achievement in quarrying enormous blocks of granite and floating them down the Nile to build temples, tombs, furniture and colossi is staggering to contemplate. Nevertheless that feat is matched by others almost equally impressive – cities carved out of living rock, stone buildings constructed, without mortar, of slabs cut so accurately that, hundreds of years later, it is still impossible to slip a blade between them.

European stonework reached its height during the Middle Ages when superb castles and churches were built and lavishly decorated by stone carvers. The names of the craftsmen have not come down to us but some of them left their secret personal mark hidden among the curlicues. Many of the carvings were based on biblical themes, and were designed to teach the illiterate. The faces of the characters portrayed were frequently those of local merchants and craftsmen, and a few gargoyles were generally thrown in to frighten the devil's messengers. The gargoyles eventually became architectural conceits and often appeared on waterspouts, drainage pipes and above doorways.

The building of cathedrals eventually waned, but stone craftsmen continued to make bowls, mortars, tombstones and other articles, including engraved stones used in the printing process.

Today the most notable work being done in the field is being produced by the Eskimos who are famous for their soapstone carving. They are gradually moving away from the utilitarian aspect of the craft, however, and turning more and more to stone sculpture.

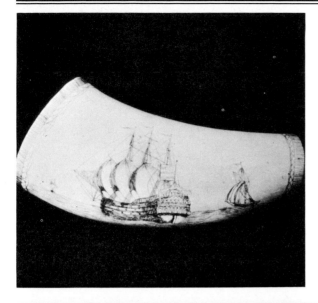

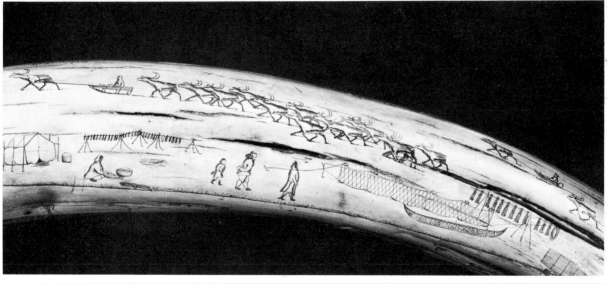

Scrimshaw. (Nova Scotia Museum Collection. Photo R. Merrick)

Ancient carved stone pipe bowl of Indian origin (Royal Ontario Museum)

Carved tusk of Eskimo origin (Royal Ontario Museum)

The cutting and polishing of precious and semiprecious stones is another important aspect of the stoneworker's craft. Lapidaries – so named from the Latin word for stone – have been working for more than six thousand years, finishing gems for inlay work and setting and incising stones for the seals which were widely used in days when few could read and stamped pictures had to serve as signatures.

Today lapidaries employ techniques that have changed little since the Assyrians invented sapphire-tipped drills that could work hard stone such as porphyry. Many of those who are active in the field at the present time, however, are hobbyists who finish native stones of all types. Few of them attempt to do the setting or designing which are now considered part of the craft, but their enthusiasm is stirring up considerable interest among the designer-artisans.

Ivory

Tradition says that Solomon's throne was made of ivory and that it was guarded by nine silver lions. By the time it was made, however, the working of ivory was an ancient art. The tusks of elephants, sea lions and other animals, as well as the ice-preserved tusks of long-extinct mammoths, have been utilized by man since prehistoric times.

Objects of ivory were made in ancient Egypt, Assyria and the Mediterranean countries. The Greeks and Romans used the material lavishly to inlay furniture and weapons, as well as to decorate sculpture which often consisted of a wooden foundation covered with layers of precious materials. The Athena of Phidias, for example, had hair of gold and face and hands of ivory.

The art of ivory carving, which was perfected by the Chinese, Japanese and Indians, was taken to the West by the Moors who also transported the game of chess with its traditional ivory men. Perhaps because of its proximity to Africa, the prime source of ivory, the Mediterranean coast soon became the centre for ivory carving. From there the craft spread north, and in the Middle Ages ivory was used extensively in the great churches of Europe. Liturgical objects such as reliquaries, screens, plaques, diptyches and book covers were made of ivory and small carved ivory statues were common. Unfortunately the craft declined during the fifteenth century and in the Western world it never reached such heights again.

Cutting stones in convex form and polishing (but not faceting) them is one of the easiest of the lapidary arts. The cabochons, as they are called, are inexpensive to produce, and they afford the craftsman a good opportunity to select interesting material. The first step is to outline the gem on a precut slab. The "blank" is then sawed out roughly, trimmed down in several stages, ground down to shape, then sanded and polished on a revolving wheel.

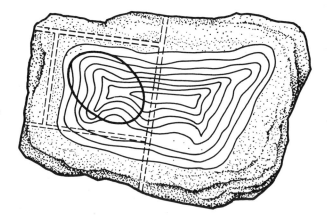

Ivory carving did not completely die out, however; it became the craft of sailors. They had few tools – usually only a knife and sometimes an adze – but they managed to cut, carve and incise whalebone, shark and whale teeth and walrus tusks during their long watches. The objects they made – corset stays, rattles, powderhorns and buttons – were usually small so that they could be packed away in their gear to be used for gifts when land was reached.

The ivory carving done by the sailors is known as "scrimshaw" though no one knows exactly why. Some folklorists suggest that the word may come from the Dutch *skrimsharder*, "a lazy fellow" – which ties in with the fact that it was a leisure-time occupation.

It is interesting to note that the Alaska Eskimos, who are famous carvers and shrewd traders, also produce ivory pieces that are very similar to scrimshaw.

Very little ivory carving is being done today. The material is both scarce and expensive and the medium seems to offer little to the contemporary craftsman who wants to be freed from the constraints of limited space and minute detailing.

Horn

Horn is a tough, hard substance which forms on the outside of the bony core projecting from the head of hoofed animals. In many cultures it is believed to be an aphrodisiac as well as an antidote to poison.

Horns, which in religious and art connotations are regarded as symbols of power, have over the years served many purposes. From early times they have been used as drinking cups, particularly by the mead and beer drinkers of northern Europe, and it was the fact that a horn rolls when it is put down that led to the custom of drinking a full measure without pausing. They have also been used as containers for gunpowder, and in this role they have become inextricably linked in the minds of many people with the pioneer days in North America.

The ram's horn, which still sounds the traditional religious call of the Jews, is just one application of the horn as a musical instrument. It was also employed, in the early days, for warning ships during fogs. And its name is perpetuated in both musical and navigational terminology.

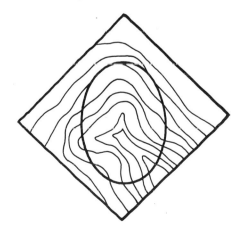

Horn spoons still appear frequently on breakfast tables in Scottish communities, and combs, buckles, buttons and book covers were at one time made of the substance.

Children of the sixteenth century were taught their alphabets from a horn book – a paddle-shaped board to which was affixed a printed sheet protected by a layer of transparent horn. This same transparent material was once extensively used as a glass substitute, particularly for lanterns.

Today few craftsmen work in horn, which is rapidly being replaced by the glass, metal and plastics which are cheaper and more abundant.

Textile Patterning

Batik by Elaine Walker-Fogg, Calgary, Alberta

Batik

"Batik" is a Malaysian word describing an age-old method of patterning textiles by applying a "resist" which prevents dye from penetrating certain areas of the cloth. The craft reached its highest development in Java, and the work done there influenced batiking throughout the Orient, Africa and India. The Dutch colonizers of Java introduced the process to Europe in the middle of the seventeenth century and from there it spread into England.

The English and other textile-producing nations undertook the mass production of imitation batik in the mid-nineteenth century, but the operation required more complicated machinery than that used for printed textiles, and proved to be an extremely expensive one. Nevertheless machine-made batiks were produced and sold in limited quantity until early in the twentieth century, when the textile industry was beset by economic difficulties that spelled the end of the factory-made product.

In the meantime, however, Western craftsmen had taken to the art and were turning out highly detailed and over-decorated batiks. The Germans were particularly enthusiastic, and were producing elaborately patterned gowns – and curtains which looked very much like stained glass since some wax was purposely left on the fabric.

The trend to ornateness was reversed in 1900 when Javanese dancers wearing traditional costumes toured Europe. Suddenly Western craftsmen saw batik as it was originally conceived – simply designed but intricately coloured. They proceeded then to produce pieces that showed fresh inspiration and greater vitality.

Following World War II batik again experienced a renaissance, no doubt because many Europeans returning from the Orient brought with them samples of Indonesian batik which was at the time undergoing a government-sponsored revival. The interest in the craft continued, and at the present time batik is receiving a great deal of attention from craftsmen. This is largely due to the fact that present-day fabrics are easier to dye than they were a decade ago; they resist shrinking and fading, absorb dyes more readily, and give more predictable results. It is also due to the fact that dyes are now simpler to mix, come in a wide variety of colours, and are relatively permanent.

The basic process of making batiks remains the same now as when the craft originated, however. The areas of the textile that are to remain free from dye are covered with a dye-resistant substance (usually wax). The fabric is then dyed either by dipping it into a dye bath or by brushing dye over the uncoated areas. That done, the resist is removed with heat, solvents or by scraping. The result is a single-colour pattern on a plain or coloured ground.

If more than one colour is desired the three steps are gone through again. Other areas of the pattern are blocked out with the resist, another dye is applied, and a two-colour design is achieved. (The effect, however, may be of a three-colour pattern, since previously dipped, unwaxed portions of the design will take on a colour that is a combination of the two dyes.)

For each additional colour the process is repeated. In the case of very intricate designs as many as twenty separate waxing and dyeing operations may be required, but two or three are usual. Javanese batiks are made with a limited number of natural dyes – usually not more than two or three, selected from indigo, red, brown and yellow – but they are applied in many successive stages, to produce subtle, decorative effects. A traditional sarong may take up to fifteen days to produce.

The craftsmanship rests in applying the resist, rather than in the dyeing. The simplest method consists of outlining the design with a pen-like implement, which deposits hot wax in a controllable stream. Once the edges have been covered, the rest of the area to be reserved is quickly waxed with a brush. At one time an attempt was made by the Germans to electrify the waxing tool but today most craftsmen use manual tools.

There are many variations of the basic method, of course, and many contemporary craftsmen have worked out their own techniques for creating batik. The resist, for example, need not be wax. The Chinese use a soya-bran cheese formula for the blue-and-white patterned fabrics they batik. In other countries cassava starch serves the same purpose. Some craftsmen employ stencils in the application of the resist, and in Java, for "economy" batiks, the wax is put on with the help of blocks that have been dipped in liquid wax.

The "crackle," or veining, which is characteristic of traditional batik, results when the cooled wax cracks and the dye penetrates. Today it is possible to make batik without the crackle, since the new resists are very flexible, and many craftsmen choose to do so. Others, however, prefer to retain the veining and deliberately crumple the material to achieve the effect.

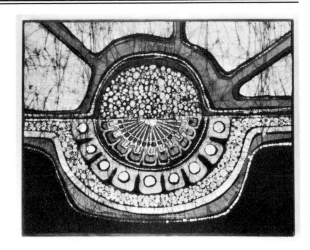

Batik in red tones by Judy Pisano, Toronto, Ontario

Batik by Sandra Tivy, Calgary, Alberta

"Washing Line Number 1," batik hanging by Jill Maycock, Lambeth, Ontario

"The Green Wizard," mixed media marionette by Sandra Tivy, Calgary, Alberta

In other ways, too, the contemporary craftsman working with batik may follow his own bent rather than traditional methods. Designs are freer and bolder today than in earlier times. The choice of materials is wider; leather, synthetic fabrics and paper, as well as cotton and silk, are batiked. Colours are more vibrant, and the wider range of synthetic dyes now available makes it possible for the designer to create what are, in effect, works of art – unique expressions of his individuality.

The "resist" process is also used in the dyeing of Easter eggs, an old craft that was carried on in the Ukraine before the Christian era and that is widely practised in Canada today. The design is painted on the egg with a fine-pointed stylus, the areas to be exempted from the dye are waxed, and the egg (which may be cooked, raw or blown, and in some cases is made of wood) is dipped in Colour Number One. The wax is then removed, replaced on other areas, and the egg redipped. It's the batik procedure exactly.

The patterns used for Easter eggs are highly symbolic, with heavy emphasis on geometrics and stylized plants. They are the old designs which relate to the folklore surrounding the craft, and the belief that a decorated egg will ensure a good harvest and avert evil.

Tie-dye

It is thought that tie-dyeing originated in China and spread from there throughout the world, acquiring special attributes in each country. In India it was characterized by a repetition of circular patterns, from tiny dots to large whorls. (The small dots were made by girls with very long nails on their thumbs and forefingers who picked up minute points of material for binding.) In Japan the method was used to decorate the luxurious native silks, and was reserved for the use of the priests and nobility. In Africa the patterns were bolder and the materials heavier, but the techniques were obviously the same as those practised in Asia.

It is not known exactly when the craft spread to the Western world, but it is probable that the activities of the large trading companies, notably the East India Company, stimulated interest among the Europeans, and in due course the Spanish, French and English practised the art in the New World.

They were not the first to do so, however. There is evidence that the South American Indians used the tie-dye method to decorate fabrics in a pre-Columbian era, and that at a later time Indian tribes further north – notably the Pueblo and the Hopi – also made use of the technique.

Wherever it is practised, the tie-dye method is basically the same. The fabric is tied, knotted, bound, folded, pleated and stitched in a variety of ways, with string, rubber bands, or any other material that will resist dye. The tied fabric is then immersed in dye, the bindings are removed, and the pattern emerges. Sometimes the fabric is retied and redipped a number of times, to create variations, sometimes only parts of the fabric are dipped, and sometimes rice, seeds, stones, beads or other articles are tied in to produce special effects. The fabric can also be clamped between wood and metal shapes. The possibilities are limitless.

The texture of the cloth, the "resist" qualities of the material used to tie the cloth, and the combinations of colours used are what determine the effectiveness of the finished product.

There are variations on the basic method, of course. One of these, known as ikat, is a Malaysian adaptation in which the yarn is tied and dyed before it is woven. Depending on the elasticity of the yarn and the tension used in weaving, ikat will result in an over-all tweedy blend or – if the dye has been strictly controlled – in a pattern.

Another variation is the discharge process – a method of decorating textiles very popular among young people who use it to individualize their mass-produced shorts and jeans. It consists of immersing a dark material, waxed or tied, in a bleaching solution. Provided the textile can withstand the chemical effects of the bleach, the results are sometimes quite pleasing. These same young people, stimulated by their present fascination with Eastern culture, are practising other forms of tie-dye as well, and are largely responsible for the current widespread interest in the art.

Craftsmen today have adopted the discharge method, as well as the other forms of tie-dye, and, influenced by the brilliant colours and exotic designs produced by African craftsmen, are experimenting with new elaborations of a frequently surprising and always fascinating theme.

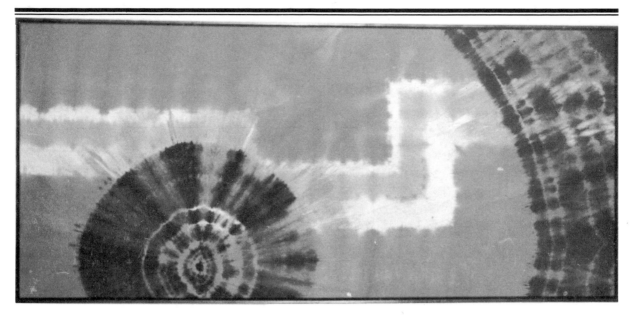

Examples of tie-dye by Eric Nyros, Clarkson, Ontario

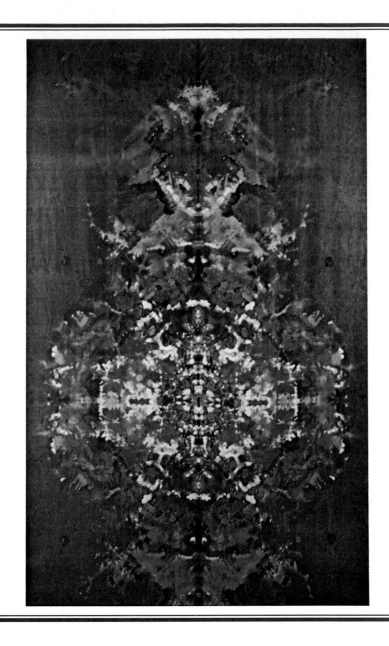

Silk banner patterned by chemical calligraphic method by Richard Hunter, Victoria, British Columbia*

Silk-screening

One of the best and most easily controlled ways to pattern textiles is to print them. There are various methods of doing this, the oldest being block printing, which was developed in China before letterpress printing came into existence in the West.

Block printing consists of a simple – though painstaking – process of transferring colour to cloth by means of wooden blocks carved in high relief. A separate block must be used for each colour, and great care must be taken to assure that the blocks are imposed correctly and that the pressure is evenly applied.

It was from this technique that the machine printing of textiles evolved. The wooden blocks were replaced by steel engravings, and these eventually were made in roller form, so that they could print continuous patterns at high speed. Since then, of course, textile printing has moved on to more sophisticated technology but some craftsmen still practise the old method of hand-printing textiles with wooden blocks. They find that the subtle effects so achieved reward them for the time and patience expended.

Most craftsmen today prefer to print textiles by the silk-screen process, however. Silk-screening is, basically, an extension of stencilling which has been practised from prehistoric days and is still being very creatively done, especially by the Eskimos, as mentioned in the section on appliqué.

One of the great difficulties of working with stencils is keeping the "floating" areas (those not attached to the mother stencil) in position. The first solution to this was to incorporate "bridges" into the design, so that no matter how involved a cut-out stencil might be, it all hung together.

Many artists found the bridges limiting, however, and they constantly sought ways to do away with them. The Japanese finally solved the problem by attaching the floating portions to the mother stencil with a web of hair so fine that it scarcely showed in the print. The next step was to fasten the stencil itself to a frame with a similar web. This was a great advantage, since the frame simplified the positioning of the stencil.

Gradually further refinements were added, and in 1907 a patent was issued in England for a method of making prints by forcing ink through a mesh screen with a stiff brush. Printers in the United States soon realized the commercial possibilities in this invention, and in turn, introduced an improvement – the squeegee roller which presses the ink

Both textiles and paper may be printed with wood or linoleum blocks. For this the block is carved away in all areas save those that are to appear in the print. Ink or paint is rolled on to the relief surface, the paper or cloth is lowered on to it, and pressure is applied. The print is then lifted off the block, as shown, and is allowed to dry. Usually a separate impression is made for each colour. This involves making a special block for every one.

*"Ode to Eddy," silk-screen yardage by Sheila
Skye Morrison, Toronto, Ontario*

*Eskimo printing: "Tallulyuk," sea goddess by
Paulassie, Cape Dorset, Northwest Territories*

*Eskimo printing: "The Archer," by Niviaksiak,
Cape Dorset, Northwest Territories*

through the mesh so that it covers all areas of the cloth or paper except those blocked out by the stencil.

From such a simple device a thriving industry has developed, and though craftsmen were at first slow to accept the medium, it has opened new avenues for the textile worker. The craft offers ample scope for creativity. Since a separate stencil must be made for each colour, the combinations can be varied. The imposition can be altered. And the pattern may either be repeated at length, to create a great deal of yardage, or used for limited, signed, reproductions.

Traditionally silk and cotton have been most frequently used for silk-screen patterning, but almost any textile is suitable. Colour and tone will vary with the texture of the cloth, and the craftsman's choice of material will depend upon the effect he wishes to achieve.

Contemporary designs have changed a great deal since the Asian people first experimented with textile stencilling. From graceful arabesques and intricate, symbolic designs, craftsmen have moved to bolder patterns, generally free-flowing and often abstract.

Weaving

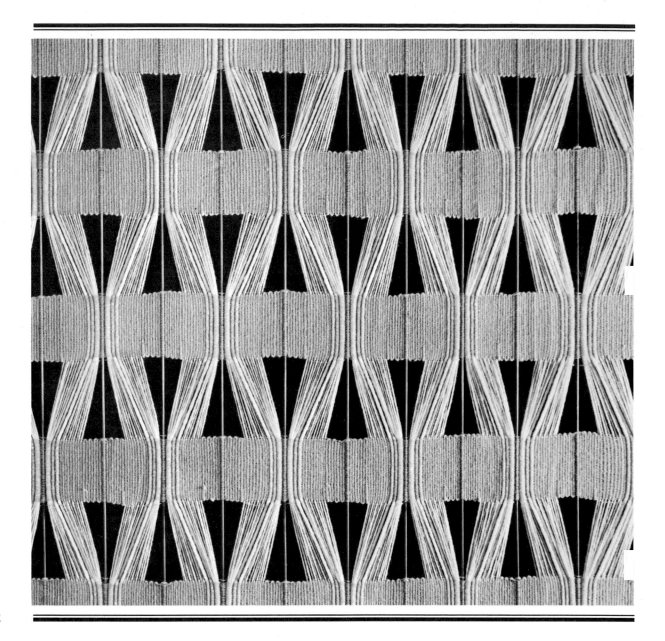

Woven screen by Velta Vilsons, Toronto, Ontario

The roots of weaving can be traced as far back in man's history as the New Stone Age, when people in many parts of the world discovered that by interlacing strips of flexible materials, a mat, or fabric, could be produced. The first weavers worked with natural substances such as grasses, vegetable fibres, barks and rawhide. But it was not long before the art of spinning was developed, and since then most fabrics have been woven with threads of flax, wool, silk and cotton.

Weaving today is based on the same principle as when it was first conceived. Woven goods, whether they are products of the hand or power loom, are made by working lengthwise strands (the "warp") into crosswise strands (the "weft," or the "woof"). The warp is stretched lengthwise to form a structure into which the weft strands are introduced in accordance with a selected pattern, or "weave." The resulting fabric, the "web", is usually pliable, but weavers have also produced stiff webs of wire, wood, metal, plastic and other unconventional materials.

The earliest weaving was done by hand, the weaver picking up every other warp strand with his fingers and inserting the weft. Before long, however, people began to experiment with devices which would keep the warp strands taut, to facilitate the interweaving. At first they simply looped the warp strands over a tree branch and let them dangle. Later, they hung weights on the ends, or tied them to a heavy pole. From this arrangement the first elementary loom developed. It consisted of two vertical sticks which supported a horizontal rod to which the warp yarns were attached. Later a second rod was added to anchor the bottom ends of the warp.

The next significant change in weaving came with the introduction of a hand-operated device for raising or lowering certain warp yarns only, leaving the others in place. This created a space called the "shed," through which the weft strands could be thrust— a great time saver. This, in turn, brought about the invention of the shuttle, a hollowed-out wooden implement which holds the weft strands so that they can easily be thrown through the open shed. This not only increased the speed of weaving; it made the production of wider fabrics possible.

Down through the centuries many types of loom have been developed. Weavers of ancient Greece preferred the upright loom on which they wove from the top down, as do some North American Indians today. Egyptian weavers adopted another type of vertical loom, one that later found favour in Persia and Scandinavia. In many countries of Central and South America, a horizontal loom, initiated by the Incas, is still in use.

The loom that brought about the greatest revolution in the weaving industry, however, was the steam power loom invented by Edmund Cartwright in 1785. Its appearance marked the beginning of the end for the home industry and the itinerant craftsman.

Developments in weaving were paralleled by advances in spinning. From the ancient method of making thread by twining fibres together with the fingers, man advanced to using a spindle, a smooth stick about a foot long, notched at one end and weighted at the other with a disk called the "whorl."

The spinner fastened one end of a thread to the stem of the spindle, and caught a loop of it in the notch at the top. She set the spindle twirling and commenced feeding fibres on to the end of the thread. The fibres were twisted and drawn out. The spun yarn was then wound on the spindle. Later a second stick, the distaff, was also employed. It was generally about three feet long, and served to hold the unspun fibres.

The next advance was the spinning wheel, which came into use in Europe around the fourteenth century. The spindle now hung horizontally in a frame and was revolved by means of a driving belt that passed over a wheel. The wheel was at first turned by hand and later by a foot treadle.

The spinning wheel was modified and improved many times over the years. In the mid-eighteenth century James Hargreaves invented the spinning jenny which could spin a number of threads at a time. A few years later James Arkwright brought out a frame which, by means of rollers, pulled out the yarn, twisted and wound it, all in one operation. At first the frame was run by horse or mule effort, later by water power, and eventually by steam. Arkwright's machine and a subsequent one invented by Samuel Crompton heralded the commencement of the factory and the decline of spinning as a routine household chore.

The art of dyeing also progressed to keep pace with developments in the production of cloth. For a long time it did not occur to spinners and weavers to treat threads or fabrics with dye. As they became increasingly conscious of the aesthetic value of their craft, however, they began to experiment with vegetable dyes made from bark, berries and roots of various plants. Later they found that dyes made from certain insects and shellfish were also effective, and that some minerals could be used as mordants, or fixatives, to

154

The wool wheel, also called the walking wheel, was operated by hand. The spindle was turned by means of a driving belt which passed over the wheel. The spinner walked backward to draw out the fleece and forward to wind it on the spindle. The smaller wheel was worked with foot treadles, and the spinner could sit as she worked. It was used chiefly for cotton and flax.

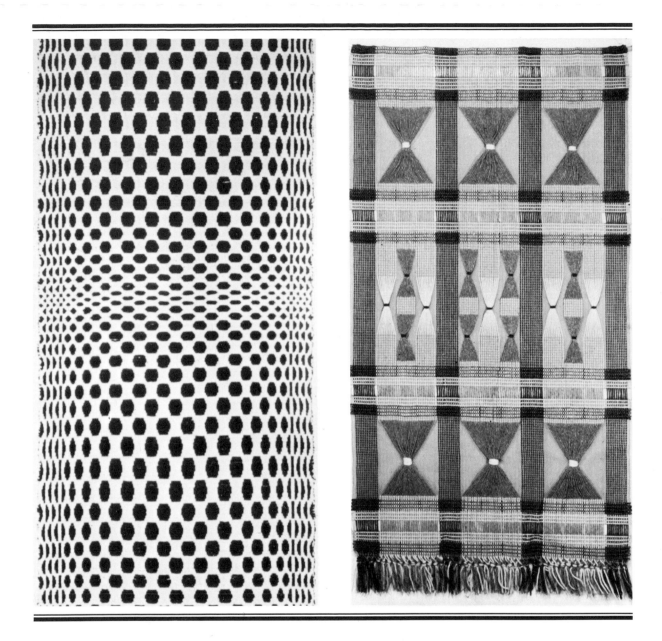

Wall hanging, "Opt Illusion," by Laura Peachell, Guelph, Ontario*

Woven wall hanging by Velta Vilsons, Toronto, Ontario*

Woven space hanging in sprang technique by Marie Aiken, Gravenhurst, Ontario

"Rusalkad," three-dimensional wall hanging by Jana Kavan Nor, Downsview, Ontario

make the dyes permanent. As the demand for coloured fabrics increased, dyeing became an industry in its own right, and dyeworks sprang up in all the important textile centres.

In the mid-nineteenth century chemical dyes were discovered, and since then they have been used almost exclusively, though of recent years designers have tended to turn back to the soft, earthy tones obtainable only from pure plant dyes.

In North America the art of weaving was already old in history by the time the white man arrived. The explorer Simon Fraser recorded in his journal in 1808, "They [the Indians] make rugs of dog-hair, which have strips of different colours crossing at right angles ressembling a Scottish plaid. . . ."

The newcomers soon recognized the exceptional skill of the native people in this, as well as other crafts. Indian tribes in the southwest, notably the Navajos, wove textiles on looms. In other areas less sophisticated techniques were employed, but some of the fabrics produced were very handsome.

Indian weavers used the hair of buffalo, moose, and mountain goat, and in some areas dogs were raised especially for their hair. Leather thongs, rawhide and coarse grasses also served and vegetable fibres, such as Indian hemp, nettles, milkweed, and the inner bark of softwood trees such as cedar and basswood, were spun by hand or on a spindle into threads of suitable length.

The oldest form of Indian weaving was done on the fingers. Threads were wound between the fingers and then looped over one another to make a web. On occasion, a needle or a hook was used to manipulate the threads, and sometimes a frame was employed. Variations of this process of looping are still practised. Corkwork, or spool knitting, is a direct descendant.

Finger weaving of various types was originally done by Indians all across the continent, but in Canada it reached its zenith on the Pacific coast. The Salish tribes of southern British Columbia, the Tshimsian in the northern part of the province, and the Tlingit in the Alaskan panhandle brought the technique to the heights of fine art, producing blankets and other articles of superb craftsmanship.

The Salish were also noted for their loom weaving. The frame they used consisted of two cedar posts set firmly in an earth floor about six feet apart, and slotted to support two horizontal rollers. The warp of wool, animal hair or plant fibre was wound around the rollers, and the weft was interlaced by hand. Like other Indian tribes, the band had its

One of the oldest known looms is the vertical loom in which the warp threads are hung from a tree branch or horizontal rod and weighted at the bottom. The weaving is done by inter-lacing the weft threads with the fingers. Some very sophisticated weaving has been done by this method. The Salish Indians, in particular, were at one time extremely skilled in the art, and produced blankets famous for their beauty and durability. The craft is now being revived.

own traditional textile patterns, similar to those used in their basket weaving.

Natural substances provided the Indians with a wide range of dyes. Alder bark produced a rose colour, lichens gave a yellow. Cedar and hemlock bark were used for browns, Oregon grape for a yellow-green, and copper for blue-green. Iron and lime were used as fixatives.

The Salish considered blankets symbols of wealth, and often presented them as gifts on ceremonial occasions. A Salish bride of rank might walk on a pathway of beautiful, soft-hued blankets from her home to her husband's canoe.

By the beginning of the twentieth century, however, the tradition of blanket-making began to die. Because the Hudson's Bay Company offered one brightly coloured commercial blanket in exchange for sixty salmon, the Indians were lured away from their looms, and eventually lost their skill. Today the only large collections of Salish blankets are located in museums. It is comforting to know that of recent years a few of the women have gone back to weaving, and some belts, back straps and rugs are being made once more.

When the white settlers first came to Canada all the processes involved in the making of cloth were done at home, from the growing of the flax and the raising of the sheep to the finishing of the yard goods.

Because there was no other light-weight weaving material available at the time, flax was one of the first crops to be planted in the New World. It was easy to grow but, once harvested, it had to be extensively treated before it could be woven. The seeds had to be removed, and it had to be retted, or soaked, then dried and beaten with mallets. And finally the long fibres had to be combed. It was a laborious, time-consuming business.

The raising of the sheep was no easy task either, in a country where there were so many predators and where it was so difficult to obtain the fresh stock necessary to keep the flocks from degenerating. Moreover, the sheep had to be washed and sheared; the fleece had to be scoured to cleanse it and remove excess oil, and then it had to be carded, or combed, to straighten and separate the fibres.

The next step was the spinning. This was a familiar chore to the pioneers who were accustomed to making their own cloth. Every settler's home had a spinning wheel, and some households had two, a large wheel for wool, and a smaller one that could be used for both flax and wool.

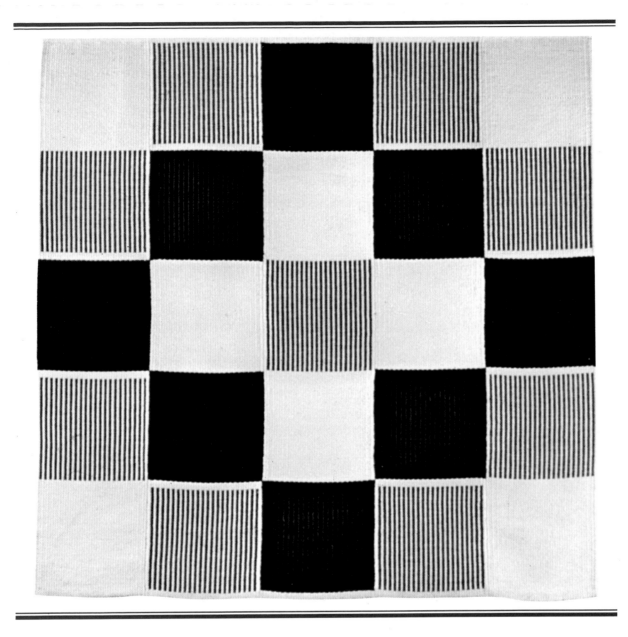

"Plan No. 1," woven wall hanging by Elin Corneil, Toronto, Ontario*

At first the spinning wheels were made by hand, often by the settler himself. By the 1860's, however, advertisements for commercially made wheels were appearing. In 1866 *The Canada Farmer* advertised "Del's Lever Spinning Wheel," priced at $7.50 – a large sum in those days. But the wheel was a worthwhile investment for those who could afford it, because it had a long arm which moved back and forth, permitting the spinner to sit while at work. It must have been a boon to the women who had covered as much as twenty miles a day spinning with the wool wheel (also aptly called the "walking wheel"), moving back to draw out the fleece, then forward to wind the spun yarn onto the spindle.

The dyeing was generally done when the yarn had been spun, and the dye substances were those traditionally used by the Indians. Goldenrod, which produced a soft yellowish-brown, and bloodroot, which gave a pleasing red, were special favourites.

The weaving was done according to traditional practices which the settlers had brought with them from their homelands. Each district had its own particular weaves and patterns. The Acadians, for example, produced textiles that were firmly woven, with the wool weft so tight that the warp could not be seen.

The Québecois were famous for their wide, brightly coloured sashes (called ceintures fléchées because of their typical arrow-head motifs) which were diagonally plaited and interwoven in a technique reminiscent of work done by the Indians before the advent of the white man. They were made and worn by both the habitants and the Indians, and it is a matter of conjecture which group they originated with. Certainly the French colonists did imitate the Indians in many ways: in their use of canoes, corn, maple, herbal remedies, and in their general adaptation to their environment. Peter Kalm, a Swedish scientist who visited Canada in 1749, wrote: "Whereas many nations imitate French customs, I notice that here it is the French who, in various respects, imitate the customs of the Indians with whom they are in daily contact. They smoke, in Indian pipes, tobacco prepared in the native way; they wear shoes in the Indian fashion, and garters and sashes like the Indians."

Whatever their origin, the sashes became very popular with the French Canadians, and served as the basis for a Quebec cottage craft that flourished from around 1830 to 1860. The weavers did not vary the design or colours of these "trade sashes" very much. They were generally red, light blue, dark blue, yellow and green, and unlike the traditional sashes, were made in narrow widths, never more than six inches across. They were sold cheaply

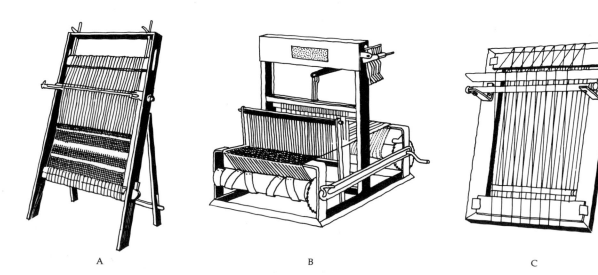

A   B   C

and in great quantities by the Hudson's Bay Company until the demand became so great that mechanically woven sashes were imported from England – whereupon the home industry vanished.

Hand-woven ceintures fléchées did not entirely disappear, however. At the end of the nineteenth century it became fashionable among the bourgeoisie to wear immense fringed sashes over winter coats, and some very handsome specimens were produced. Eventually this fad too died out, but in 1907 the Canadian Handicraft Guild arranged an exhibition and demonstration of ceintures fléchées at the Art Gallery of Montreal, and this in turn led to a revival of interest in the craft.

Other weavers in various parts of the country had their own special textures and patterns. Linsey-woolsey, a mixture of linen and wool, was a favourite with all the home weavers and was generally produced in stripes of different widths and colours.

When it was woven the fabric had to be shrunk, or fulled, before it could be made up. In many areas this was the excuse for a bee, and all the neighbours would come to help. Songs were sung with a strong, rhythmic beat as teams of men and women twisted and pulled the dampened cloth.

As the country opened up, the tasks of the home weaver became easier. Some of the processes were taken over by professionals. The dyeworks might colour the wool, or the finished cloth might go to the mill for a final gloss finish or to be shrunk. Cotton produced by mills in New England could by then be purchased in skeins from general stores – except during the Civil War when the cotton industry in the United States was paralyzed.

By this time some of the weaving might be sent out to people who made a business of the craft. The professional weavers produced clothing material, blanketing, bedcovers, table linen, and yards of striped carpeting. Many of the later settlers had served tough apprenticeships in Europe and had acquired sophisticated skills. The Germans who settled in Lunenberg County, Nova Scotia and in southern Ontario were particularly adept. They made colourful checked blankets, usually red and blue, and reversible summer-weight coverlets with one side light, the other dark. They also made doublecloth coverlets – two independent layers of cloth – one wool, the other cotton – woven simultaneously.

Once begun, the industrialization of textile manufacture accelerated rapidly. Spinning

Simple frame looms (A and B) are operated by weaving the weft threads in and out with the fingers or by lifting alternate warp threads with a shed stick. Table looms (C) are more complicated. They are operated by raising and lowering, by hand, harnesses which manipulate the warp threads. There are usually several harnesses, which makes it possible to do intricate weaves. Floor looms (D) are similar, but the harnesses are operated with foot treadles.

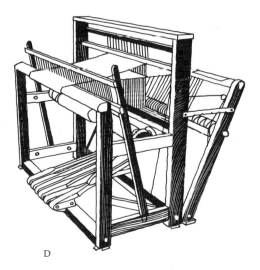

D

and weaving mills were established. By 1851 there were eighteen woolen mills in operation in Canada East and seventy-four in Canada West. And in 1865 there were five cotton mills operating, producing sheeting, shirting, yarn, bags and other merchandise. In the end, the weaving of carpets was the last stand of the professional hand weavers who could no longer compete with mass production.

Weaving and spinning in the home has continued as a craft, however, particularly in Quebec. In that province it was revived, prior to the 1837 uprising, as a protest against the import of British goods, and when it began to die out in the 1930's it was stimulated once again by the provincial government. It has flourished ever since, and the work being done in the province today is outstanding.

In other parts of Canada the popularity of craft weaving is increasing. There is a revival in the making of traditional coverlets, and some of those being produced in the Maritimes and Ontario can scarcely be told from heirloom pieces. At the same time there is much experimental work being done. Designer-craftsmen are creating interesting textiles, using new techniques or old ones with fresh applications. They are combining fibres and colours in unusual ways, to produce three-dimensional hangings, sculptured cloth, and heavily textured fabrics.

Tapestry

The work "tapestry" has come to have two meanings. Traditionally it is a type of weaving in which different coloured yarns are threaded into the warp, with the fingers or a bobbin, to form a picture or design. Today the word is also used to describe a piece of needlework that is completely covered with stitchery. For the purpose of this book "tapestry" is used in the traditional sense, and always — except for the Bayeux Tapestry — refers to woven work.

Traces of ancient tapestries have been found in Peru and Egypt, and Greek vases of the sixth century show horsemen wearing tapestry cloaks. Clearly, then, tapestry weaving is a very old craft, and very widespread. It is believed that it originated in the East and was carried to the West by the Arabs who, in their advances, preserved the art where they found it and introduced it into many countries where it was previously unknown, notably into North Africa and Spain.

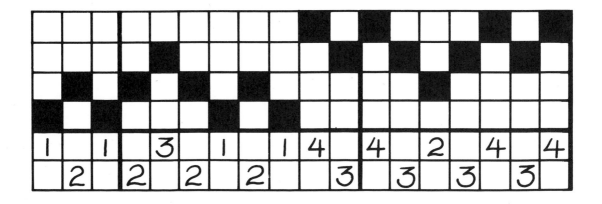

*Black wool hanging by Heidi Roukema, West Montrose, Ontario**

*A draft, or warp plan, is made to show the
threading of a loom. The vertical rows of
squares represent the warp threads, the numbers
stand for the harnesses. In this warp plan, the
first warp on the right goes through a heddle
on Harness #4, the second through one on #3, etc.*

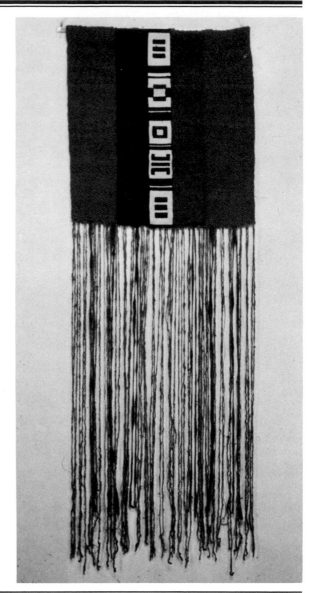

*Tapestry, "City," by Joanna Staniszkis,
Vancouver, British Columbia**

*Tapestry by Collee Foster, Don Mills,
Ontario**

The great flowering of the Church in the West gave impetus to the new style of weaving, and it is interesting to note that many of the earliest ecclesiastical tapestries show a Byzantine influence. The figures are rigid, the faces stare out with dark-rimmed, almond-shaped eyes.

Apart from the Church, only the very wealthy could afford the luxury of such laboriously woven pieces. They were reserved for kings and nobles, who used them as wall coverings, carpets and bed furnishings. The hangings they found particularly useful because the heavy tapestry blocked out some of the drafts in the cavernous castles. Very few of these old hangings still survive, however; the fibres were inevitably weakened by the weight of the pieces and they have long since disintegrated.

From Spain tapestry weaving spread to the Spanish Netherlands, Italy, the German states, England and France. But the most influential work was done in what is now Belgium and the Franco-Belgian frontier, particularly in Arras, Brussels and Antwerp. Later, in the seventeenth century, Paris became an important tapestry centre, and there the craft reached its highest artistry.

From this period two names stand out: Gobelin and Aubusson. The tapestries that came to be known as Gobelins were first made by two Flemings who received their letters patent from Henry IV, who lured to France many non-Catholic artisans after the Edict of Nantes. Their business flourished, and eventually they set up workshops in buildings that had belonged to the Gobelin family, who were famous cloth dyers. Later the Gobelin workshops were purchased by Louis XIV, and most of the tapestries then went directly to the royal palaces, leaving little for private purchasers. To supply the rest of the nobility, more workshops were set up, including one at Aubusson in central France. The factory at Aubusson flourishes to this day, weaving contemporary tapestry for designers from all over the world. The Gobelin workshops also continue to weave, but they adhere to classic, representational designs.

Tapestry looms differ. The Gobelin looms, for example, are upright, while the Aubusson ones are horizontal. But the basic operation is the same in all cases. Each colour runs off a separate bobbin and is worked in separately, in blocks. As a result, there are slits between the various patches of colour. Sometimes these are closed by sewing, but occasionally they are left open to give the effect of shadow when the tapestry is hung.

At one time most tapestry pieces were designed by one person and woven by another.

Most of the designers were artists and many famous painters, including Raphael, did sketches for tapestries. The weaver was an artisan who merely copied the design and made no changes. If the tapestries were very large, many weavers stood side by side and mechanically followed instructions called out by a foreman, from the designer's plan. But even if there was only one weaver he was allowed no creative leeway, and was often not even consulted regarding the technical feasibility of the design. As a result, there existed a chronic state of conflict between the designer and the artisan.

Today this situation is changing, particularly in North America. Now designers are generally qualified craftsmen as well, and frequently do their own weaving. Or, if the tapestry is very large, they act as supervisors.

Canadians are becoming well known for their tapestry, particularly for monumental works like the theatre curtains in the National Arts Centre, Ottawa and in the John F. Kennedy Center for Performing Arts in Washington, D.C. They are producing both traditional tapestries and works of contemporary design. The contemporary tapestries can be hung but are no longer necessarily flat and rug-like. Often they are three-dimensional and are combined with other fabrics — pieces of tatting, crocheting or stitchery, for example. In some cases, plastic, metal or rope may be incorporated to create unusual effects. Tapestry weaving today has become very much a matter of designer's choice.

Basket-making

The materials and methods used in basket weaving and in the weaving of textiles are often identical. In the case of basketry, however, it is usually receptacles, furniture, hats, or tools of one kind or another that are produced.

Basket making as a craft is even older than the weaving of fabrics. Ancient man wove huts which he daubed with clay to keep out the wind and rain. He made containers for food, fish traps, sieves, and many articles. The early Britons even wove a boat — the coracle — a small, broad craft constructed of wickerwork or interwoven laths covered with a waterproof layer of skin or canvas. Many primitive peoples also made woven vessels which, when coated with clay or resin, would hold water and could be used for cooking, by dropping in hot coals to boil the water. It was in containers like this that the North American Indians made maple syrup.

Hand-woven wool and sisal curtain in Shaw Festival Theatre, designed by Ray Senior, Hudson, Quebec

Ash-splint basket made by the Penobscot
Indians of eastern Canada (Royal Ontario
Museum)

Eskimo basket by Jean, Port Harrison,
Quebec *

Contemporary Black Refugee basket made in
Nova Scotia

Contemporary Mohawk basket decorated
with sweet grass

The early basket weavers used natural materials that required little preparation apart from soaking the strands to make them flexible. In the East cane and bamboo served, in Africa palm leaves and coconut fibres, in North America grasses, reeds, braided corn husks, birchbark, wood strips, willow, cane and roots. Later basket makers used materials that required special processing. They pounded wood to separate the fibres; shoots from the rattan palm were treated to produce reeds and cane; raffia was made from the fronds of a special tropical palm. These substances are still in use today, but now wire, metal, plastic strips and many other materials are also employed to achieve unusual effects.

There are three basic basket-making techniques: plaiting, twining and coiling. Plaited baskets are made by weaving one set of material into another, alternately passing the weft over and under to produce a web. Twined baskets are made by encircling each warp with two or more wefts. This holds the warps firmly in position, and results in very substantial containers. Coiled baskets are made by coiling twisted strips of fibre around in a continuous spiral and lashing them together. The majority of baskets produced by the Indians in Western Canada today are twined or coiled; those produced in Eastern Canada are generally plaited.

When factory-produced pottery, glass and plastic vessels became available, woven ones became redundant, and basket making gradually died out except in areas relatively untouched by technology. The craft continued to flourish only in remote areas of South America and Africa, in the islands of the South Pacific, in parts of China, and in North America, where the Indians and Eskimos had developed the art to a high degree.

Almost all the Indian cultural groups have practised basketry for centuries and in many areas they continue to do so. It is usually possible to tell fairly specifically where an Indian basket was made, since each tribe has its own distinctive, traditional techniques of construction and patterns of decoration. Some tribes ornament their baskets with the same quill-work embroidery they use for their birchbark boxes. Some employ dyed grasses, beads and textured loops to achieve the decorative effects they favour.

The Eskimos also produce baskets of high quality, using the grasses that grow on dunes or among the rocks, willow roots and other substances. They prefer the coiling technique, often dyeing the grasses first for a multi-colour effect. They may also introduce strips of sealskin or other materials and occasionally individual touches, such as carved knobs on basket lids. But usually the construction and embellishment of their baskets follows the

SOME SIMPLE BASKET WEAVES

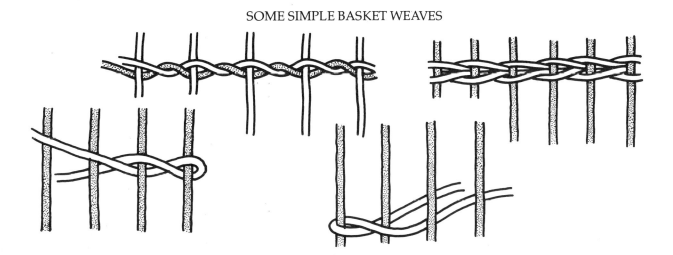

age-old patterns established in their own particular locality.

Another type of basket is currently being made in Canada. This is the Preston or black refugee basket of Nova Scotia, which originated with the slaves who escaped to Canada during the War of 1812 and took up land in the Preston area. The traditional African basket-making skills which the refugees brought with them have been practised ever since – handed down from generation to generation.

Preston baskets, which are made of split maple, are woven by the women of wood collected and prepared by the men. It is interesting to note, however, that the preparation does not include the usual step of soaking the weft strips to make them pliable. These baskets are easily identifiable because of their distinctive boat-like shape. The ribs are fastened together at one point, splay out from there, and come together again directly opposite the starting point. They were originally left in their natural colour or tinted with vegetable dyes. Today the makers of Preston baskets use very bright commercial dyes and the result is sometimes less pleasing then the soft-hued baskets of former days.

Apart from the work of the Preston weavers and that of the Indians and Eskimos, there is not much basketry being done in Canada today. Those who are carrying on the craft are experimenting with unusual materials and are producing novel articles in a variety of shapes. But, generally speaking, the contemporary craftsmen working in this field seem to find little inspiration in the medium.

Woodwork

With the help of such primitive tools as wedges and hammers, prehistoric man was able to build wooden shelters, sea-going boats, furniture and household utensils. All woodworking since that time has been a development and refinement of the basic processes he employed.

The discovery that tools could be made of metal was a major breakthrough. The invention of saws and knives made it possible to split wood into boards which could be fastened together with nails or interlocking joints, to construct substantial objects.

As more sophisticated tools were developed, articles could be made that had not only stability and practicality but beauty as well. Man began to use woodworking as an outlet for creative instincts, and the Church and nobility encouraged the craft. Architectural trim, altars, reliquaries, coffers, chairs and beds of state, and many other wooden articles were turned out by master craftsmen.

From this emphasis on the adornment of buildings grew the refinement of wood carving. The first attempts were crude religious symbols, usually representing the sun. Later craftsmen were able to carve portraits, work wood to imitate linen and other textiles, and make exquisite representations of fruits and flowers. Sculpture included saints and cherubs, candlesticks, screens and friezes showing contemporary life. Practical articles such as spoons and porridge bowls were also made by wood carvers, as were dolls and puppets, which often had articulated limbs.

Musical instruments were made out of wood as well. The simplest of these were the whistle and the primitive bamboo flute. More sophisticated were the recorders so beloved of the Elizabethans. But the most glorious of all wooden instruments was the violin that reached its golden age in the sixteenth century. The centre of the violin craft was in northern Italy, in the neighbourhood of Cremona. There the greatest violins of all time were made, many of them produced by the famous Stradivari family. Other violins of great quality were crafted in Austria and France, however. And many are so made today. Indeed, the making of musical instruments has remained largely a hand operation, and some fine pieces are being produced in Canada at the present time.

Not long after the woodworking profession emerged, the workers set themselves up in trade guilds which eventually became very powerful. The labour surplus in Europe made apprenticeship necessary. It was also an advantage for the master craftsman, since it placed him in a very strong position. He had social prestige second only to the silversmith, and

172

Carved wooden musk-oxen of curly birch with cast bronze horns by Leo Gervais, Laval, Quebec.

he was able to demand payment from the parents of a prospective pupil over whom he would exercise complete authority.

There were different guilds for the various branches of woodworking, and one of these eventually became the guild of printers. From the fifteenth century printers were cutting patterns into wood blocks to make book illustrations, pictures and playing cards. This craft continued until the twentieth century.

As life became less primitive and religion spread, the art of the woodworker flourished, reaching great heights in the decorating of churches, palaces and public buildings during the Gothic period. After the Renaissance the craft went into a slight decline, but in the eighteenth century there was a revival, initiated by the work that Grinling Gibbons did for churches designed by Christopher Wren.

This was followed by a sudden upsurge of great furniture designing – particularly in England. Thomas Chippendale, the leading cabinetmaker of the period, was possibly the greatest furniture designer who ever lived. Certainly his book of designs has had a tremendous influence on furniture-makers everywhere in the English-speaking world.

At the end of the eighteenth century, the style of Chippendale and his followers began giving way to the Classic style of Robert Adam, who was inspired by the excavations in Pompeii and the rediscovery of the ancient world of Rome and Greece. He too published books of design which were studied by craftsmen all over the world. At the same time there was a great interest in the French Directoire style of furniture espoused by the painter David.

Cabinetmakers during this period did not lack for inspiration, therefore, and because they worked in close contact with their customers their work reflected not only their own and current tastes but those of the people they were serving. They continued to flourish, with some ups and downs, until the middle of the nineteenth century. By that time the woodworking machinery, which had made its appearance some years before, was having a serious effect on furniture craftsmen, and indeed on the furniture trade in general. All at once people seemed to fall in love with machine-made monstrosities. One has only to look at the catalogue of the Great Exhibition of 1851 to see what was happening. And that was only the beginning. It was downhill all the way until William Morris and his associates, at the end of the century, tried to turn back the clock and restore the purity of mediaeval craftsmanship. Though Morris' own designs did not have a wide appeal in Britain, the

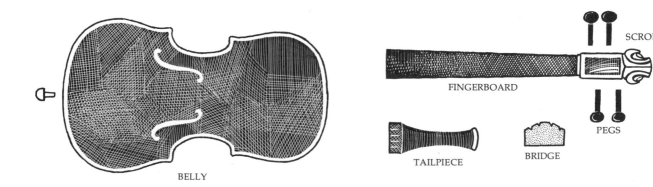

BELLY

FINGERBOARD

SCROLL

PEGS

TAILPIECE

BRIDGE

Scandinavian designers were immensely impressed by them and the inspiration that he provided started a whole new trend in furniture design.

The efforts of William Morris came too late to do much for the cabinetmakers. By that time the full force of the industrial revolution was apparent. Furniture, like other products, was being mass produced. It was, moreover, being turned out to suit the taste of the new middle class which preferred decoration above all things. Rich curlicues suggested wealth to them, and the fact that the carving was machine-made and somewhat coarse mattered not at all to the owners.

At the same time a rapid growth in population created a bigger market for furniture. The remaining hand-craftsmen could no longer afford to devote themselves to turning out a few pieces of furniture for special clients. They felt impelled to swim with the tide, so they installed some woodworking machinery and began to produce in quantity. As the number of their customers grew they began to lose touch with them, and eventually they sold only through a middleman.

The first white settlers in Canada brought to the new land the various skills they had acquired in their homelands. Many of them were trained woodworkers but others had never handled tools before. The need for weatherproof shelter was urgent, however, and everyone was obliged to assist in the building of log houses and the making of implements necessary for clearing the land, cultivating it, and storing the harvested food. All the items used in and around the home, from furniture to butter churns, were made of wood, and as very little metal was available, the pioneers were forced to be inventive in their designs and construction.

The workers were further handicapped by the fact that the tools they had brought with them were unsuitable for the tasks they were called upon to do. The European axe was too small and light for the huge trees, so the settlers were forced to make their own cutting tool, a heavy, short-handled broad axe. They also produced log peelers and pitsaws, and in the course of time chisels, augers, and even the specialized tools of the cabinetmaker, shipbuilder and cooper. There was one favourable factor, however: the large trees provided broad timbers with few knots or blemishes.

As soon as the basic necessities had been looked after, the woodworkers turned their attention to the building and decorating of churches. It was clear, however, that more

The violin-maker carves the front of a violin, called the belly, from softwood, and cuts two slots in it to allow the sound to escape. He carves the back, the sides, and the head of the fingerboard from maple or sycamore. The fingerboard and the tailpiece are made of ebony. Other parts include two interior supports (one of which also conducts the sound from front to back) and the bridge, which supports the strings. The instrument is glued, not nailed, together.

workers would be required, and Bishop Laval had a number of apprentice-trained craftsmen sent out from France. There was still a dearth of skilled labour, however, and the bishop therefore set up a craft school in the Seminary of Quebec, for carpenters, carvers, joiners, masons and stone-cutters. A second school was subsequently established at Cap Tourmente. Both schools had a tremendous influence on the future of Quebec woodworking, since the students there learned and passed on enduring traditions. In the 1650's the craft guilds were established, each with its own patron – Saint Joseph for the carpenters, Sainte Anne for the woodworkers. Members were required to be religious, charitable to fellow craftsmen in need, and to maintain the "mystery" (mastery) of their craft. These fraternities not only maintained craft standards but also perpetuated French traditions.

At a later period English settlers in the Maritimes and Upper Canada encountered the same problems that the habitants had faced and solved in New France. They too were forced to make everything of wood – stumping machines, ploughs, flails, furniture. Even the first fireplaces and chimneys were constructed of wood, and it is a tribute to the ingenuity of the builders that more of them did not catch fire.

As a matter of fact, many of the wooden articles made by the pioneers were remarkably effective. Even the blemishes in the native wood were sometimes turned to good account. With very primitive knives and a great deal of persistence the burls were turned into bowls that are greatly prized today.

By the late eighteenth century people in the settled areas of eastern Canada, who because of their trade connections were now wealthy, patronized trained cabinetmakers. These worked in imported mahogany and rosewood, following regional styles based on the great European traditions as well as those developed in the United States.

As the country opened up the cabinetmakers moved west, taking with them the styles they had adopted from the books of the great designers, as well as those that had evolved in Quebec. Always, however, the styles in Canada lagged behind the fashion in the major centres of the world.

In isolated areas of Canada regional styles were developed. The Red River chair – a sturdy pine chair with a plank seat – which was first made in the Selkirk settlement of Manitoba was a case in point.

A town might boast more than one woodworking shop. From the very early period

Lacquered wooden rooster by Pat Gagnon, Toronto, Ontario

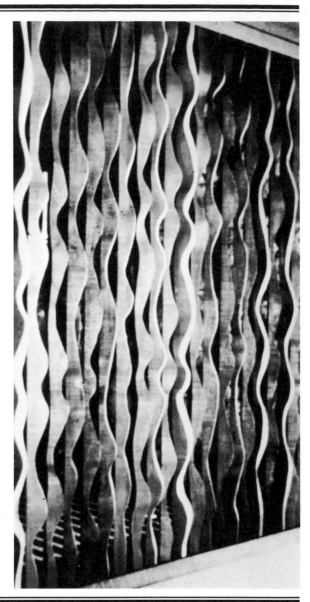

*"Eventail," fan, by Denise Beaudin,
St. Lambert, Quebec*

*Cantilevered chair in laminated cherry and
maple by Donald Lloyd McKinley,
Mississauga, Ontario*

*Wood divider by Ron Baird, Uxbridge,
Ontario (Board of Trade, Woodbridge)*

when craftsmen were doing beautiful carving for the churches of New France, to the time of the industrial revolution, there was a strong tradition of wood carving in Canada. The men who specialized in this field left their imprint on churches, public buildings, taverns and private homes. They also carved altars, candlesticks, statues, shrines and furniture, and their work, much of which was painted and gilded, brought colour and gaiety to many communities that were otherwise quite drab.

Some wood carvers became expert in carving for ships. From early times ships have been decorated with human and animal shapes, to ward off evil spirits, and the nineteenth-century sailing ships were no exception. The major piece of carving was the figurehead, the symbol of the vessel and its good luck charm. It was generally made from several pieces of wood skilfully dowelled together. The same craftsman often did scroll-work carvings for other parts of the vessel, and he might be called upon to carve huge figures representing Justice, Faith, Hope, Industry or other superhuman attributes for the top of public buildings. In slack times he might even turn out carousel animals, cigar-store Indians and tavern signs.

One step down from the carvers were the whittlers, most of whom were amateurs. Without them pioneer children would not have had toys, and square dancers would not have been able to step their paces to the tune of a fiddle, whistle or noisemaker. Checker boards, salt-shakers, boxes and candlesticks were also whittled out in leisure hours, and so were the decorated spoons which were given by young men to their girls, to mark their betrothal. (The term "spooning," as applied to courting practices, derives from this.)

By the time the highly-trained cabinetmakers arrived on the scene, most towns already had a resident woodworker. He was usually a craftsman with some training who had set up shop as a general carpenter and joiner, but who also made furniture, to order or for sale, as well as a great many other articles, including coffins as required. He did not, as a rule, attempt to produce works from the style-setters' books, but the pieces he made often displayed considerable taste and imagination.

Some towns also had a cooper who made barrels for shipping and storing all manner of goods, as well as boxes, drums and grain measures. And in many boat-building centres there were shipwrights who made scale models of ships to serve as working charts. Usually only half the model was made, since the two sides were exactly the same, but always they could be taken apart for easy examination.

SOME WOOD CHISELS AND GOUGES

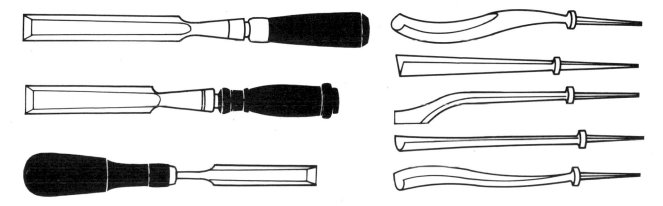

By the late nineteenth century, the pattern of life which depended on local craftsmen was beginning to change. The popular preference by then was for store-bought and catalogue items which, nine times out of ten, were machine-made. The hand-crafting of furniture gradually died out except in communities in which there were a number of Mennonites, Hutterites and Doukhoubors. They continued to make their traditional furniture which was extremely simple but beautifully constructed.

Eskimos and Indians were master woodworkers, although it is apparent that their skills deteriorated after they had contact with white traders.

Eskimo craftsmanship in general is associated with ivory and skin objects but they also worked in driftwood. Woodworking was considered a masculine craft, and the men made sleds, tools, household utensils and religious regalia (masks, rattles and drums). The woodenware was decorated with mythological creatures which placated the spirits connected with hunting, health and prosperity. These articles were made for individual and communal use, but were never sold because they were considered sacred. It was only after the decline and eventual disappearance of the Eskimo religion that wooden objects were traded, but by that time they had lost not only their symbolic meaning but their vitality. There is very little Eskimo woodwork done today.

Indians in the timber regions, notably on the west coast and in eastern Canada, worked wood with stone hammers, knives, wedges and adzes. They also knew how to hollow out trees using hot water and hot stones to soften the fibres. Wood was used for housing, and the Iroquois longhouse tribes made houses large enough for several families to live under one roof – constructed in such a way that additions could be made. The tribes without pottery used wood for everything from food containers to masks. And though the Indians initially had no horses or wheels they constructed wooden carriers to move camp equipment.

Of all the Indians those of the northwest were the most adept in handling wood. Theirs was truly a wood culture; everything was well constructed and beautifully decorated, with emphasis on mythological animals and family crests. They used wood to make raincapes, containers, bowls and platters, but they are best known for their homes, masks and totem poles. These objects represented the innermost religious philosophy of the people and their remembrance of past tribal history.

180

THE STRUCTURE OF A WHEEL

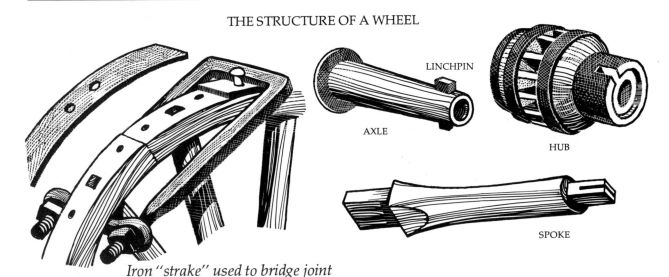

LINCHPIN

AXLE

HUB

SPOKE

Iron "strake" used to bridge joint

Iroquois war club (Royal Ontario Museum)

Ojibwa cradle board (Royal Ontario Museum)

Wood sculpture by Stephen Hogbin, Toronto, Ontario. On the left, cedar; on the right, cherry.

Because theirs was a privileged society with ranking nobility, family crests were an important part of the decoration. Much of the meaning of the decoration was known only to the carver and his patron. This is particularly true of the totem pole.

The completion of a commissioned work was the signal for a potlach ceremony. The potlaches encouraged the production of beautiful artifacts and it is no coincidence that the banning of them hastened the cultural decline of the West Coast Indians. Today there is a revival of these crafts, and in recent years totems have been carved. Young woodcraftsmen are once again carving masks and bowls, drawing on their ancient skills, and yet at the same time much of the work has a contemporary feeling that is very exciting.

The mechanization of the woodenware industry has freed the craftsman from the necessity of making utilitarian objects. He may do so if he wishes, but generally contemporary woodworkers prefer to produce articles which demand more creativity in design and workmanship.

Today many woodcraftsmen are turning out custom-designed furniture – beautiful but utilitarian storage containers, desks and chairs. Others are involved in making church furnishings, and still others in carving and whittling wood.

In carving, the current trend is to follow the natural shape and graining rather than to impose an outside design upon the wood. As a result, many of the pieces now being made are non-objective. There is an increasing use of veneer, of laminated woods, and of unusual finishes.

Some craftsmen, however, have returned to the pioneer arts, and are making simple but functional objects that complement contemporary domestic and public architecture. Many architects realize the value of wood in relation to stark façades, and are incorporating it as an integral part of their designs.

There is a tremendous range of wood, now, from which the woodworker may make a selection. He may choose to combine several types of wood, and to introduce other substances such as rope, cork, leather and plastic into his design. But because he is more limited than other craftsmen, by reason of the tools he uses and the material itself, he is apt to be somewhat traditional in his approach.

Bibliography

CERAMICS

Ball, F. C., Lovoos, J., *Making Pottery Without a Wheel.* New York: Van Nostrand Reinhold, 1965.

Collard, E., *Nineteenth-Century Pottery and Porcelain in Canada.* Montreal: McGill-Queen's, 1967.

Webster, D., *Early Canadian Pottery.* Toronto: McClelland and Stewart, 1971.

GLASS-MAKING

Kömpfer, F., Beyer, K. G., *Glass – A World History.* London: Studio Vista, 1966.

Lee, L., *Stained Glass.* London: Oxford University Press, 1967.

Stevens, G., *Canadian Glass.* Toronto: Ryerson (McGraw-Hill Ryerson), 1967.

KNITTING & KNOTTING

Harvey, V., *Macramé: The Art of Creative Knotting.* New York: Van Nostrand Reinhold, 1967.

MacKenzie, C. D., *New Design in Crochet.* New York: Van Nostrand Reinhold, 1973.

Phillips, M. W., *Creative Knitting: A New Art Form.* New York: Van Nostrand Reinhold, 1971.

Phillips, M. W., *Step-by-Step Knitting.* New York: Golden (Golden Craft Series), 1967.

Pilcher, A. M., *Macramé: A Practical Introduction.* London: G. Bell and Sons, 1972.

Short, E., *Introducing Macramé.* London: Batsford, 1970.

LEATHERWORK

Leland, C. G., *Leather Work.* New York: Pitman, 1929.

Meilach, D. Z., *Contemporary Leather: Art & Accessories – Tools & Techniques.* Chicago: Henry Regnery, 1971.

METALWORK

Bates, K. F., *The Enamelist.* New York: World Publishing, 1967.

Gentille, T., *Step-by-Step Jewelery.* New York: Golden (Golden Craft Series), 1968.

Langdon, J. E., *Canadian Silversmiths 1700-1900.* Toronto: Stinehour, 1966.

Langdon, J. E., *Canadian Silversmiths and their Marks, 1667-1867.* Lunenburg, Vermont: Stinehour, 1960.

Lister, R., *The Craftsman in Metal.* London: G. Bell and Sons, 1966.

Mackay, D. C., *Silversmiths and Related Craftsmen of the Atlantic Provinces.* Halifax: Petheric Press, 1973.

Traquair, R., *The Old Silver of Quebec.* Toronto: Macmillan, 1940.

PLASTICS

Newman, J. H., Newman, S., *Plastics for the Craftsman: Basic Techniques for Working with Plastics.* New York: Crown (Arts & Crafts Series), 1972.

RUG-MAKING

Droop, J., *Rugmaking: A Practical Introduction.* London: G. Bell and Sons, 1971.

STITCHING

Bishop, R., Safford, C. L., *America's Quilts and Coverlets as Design: A Survey of American Bedcovers*. New York: E. P. Dutton, 1973.

Clucas, J., *Your Machine for Embroidery*. London: G. Bell and Sons, 1973.

Dyer, A., Duthoit, M., *Canvas Work From the Start*. London: G. Bell and Sons, 1972.

Finley, R. E., *Old Patchwork Quilts and the Women Who Made Them*. Philadelphia: J. B. Lippincott, 1929.

Krevitsky, N., *Stitchery: Art & Craft*. New York: Van Nostrand Reinhold, 1973.

Laliberte, N., McIlhany, S., *Banners & Hangings: Design & Construction*. New York: Van Nostrand Reinhold, 1966.

Marston, D., *Patchwork Today*. London: G. Bell and Sons, 1968.

Short, E., *Embroidery & Fabric Collage*. London: Pitman, 1967.

Webster, M., *Quilts: Their Story and How to Make Them*. New York: Doubleday, 1926.

TEXTILE PATTERNING

Krevitsky, N., *Batik: Art & Craft*. New York: Van Nostrand Reinhold, 1973.

Meilach, D. Z., *Contemporary Batik & Tie-Dye*. New York: Crown (Arts & Crafts Series), 1972.

Rambosson, Y., *Les Batiks de Madame Pangon*. Paris: Charles Moreau, 1925.

Steinmann, A., *Batik – A Survey of Batik Design*. Leigh-on-Sea, England: F. Lewis, 1958.

WEAVING

Burnham, H. B., *Canadian Textiles 1700-1900*. Toronto: Royal Ontario Museum, 1965.

Burnham, H. B., Burnham, D. K., *Keep Me Warm One Night*. Toronto: University of Toronto Press, 1972.

Constantine, M., Larsen, J., *Beyond Craft: The Art Fabric*. New York: Van Nostrand Reinhold, 1973.

McDowell, G., *Ontario Handweavers and Spinners Canadian Centennial Book*. Uxbridge, Ontario: Ontario Handweavers and Spinners, 1967.

Sesrensma, W., *Tapestries*. New York: Universal, 1965.

Znamierowski, N., *Step-by-Step Weaving*. New York: Golden (Golden Craft Series), 1967.

WOODWORK

Bradshaw, A. E., *Handmade Woodwork of the Twentieth Century*. London: John Murray, 1962.

Gould, M. E., *Early American Wooden Ware*. Rutland, Vermont: Charles E. Tuttle, 1962.

MacLaren, G., *Antique Furniture of Nova Scotia Craftsmen*. Toronto: Ryerson (McGraw-Hill Ryerson), 1961.

MacLaren, G., *Woodcarvers of Nova Scotia*. Halifax: Nova Scotia Museum, 1971.

Palardy, J., *Early Furniture of French Canada*. Toronto: Macmillan, 1971.

Pinto, E. H., *Treen and Other Wooden Bygones: An Encyclopedia and Social History*. London: G. Bell and Sons, 1969.

185

Ryder, H. G., *Antique Furniture by New Brunswick Craftsmen*. Toronto: Ryerson (McGraw-Hill Ryerson), 1965.

Shackleton, P., *The Furniture of Old Ontario*. Toronto: Macmillan, 1973.

Willcox, D., *Wood Design*. New York: Watson-Guptill, 1968.

CRAFTS OF THE INDIANS AND ESKIMOS

Barbeau, M., *Pathfinders in the North Pacific*. Toronto: Ryerson (McGraw-Hill Ryerson), 1958.

Canadian Eskimo Art. Ottawa: Queen's Printer for the Department of Northern Affairs and National Resources, 1954.

Dickason, O. P., *Indian Arts in Canada*. Ottawa: Information Canada for the Department of Indian Affairs and Northern Development, 1973.

Dockstader, F., *Indian Art in North America*. Toronto: McClelland and Stewart, 1961.

Feder, N., *Two Hundred Years of North American Indian Art*. New York: Praeger, 1972.

Jeness, D., *Indians of Canada*. Ottawa: National Museum of Canada, 1932.

Masterpieces of Indian and Eskimo Art from Canada. Ottawa: Information Canada for the National Gallery of Canada, 1969.

People of the Potlatch. Vancouver: The Vancouver Art Gallery, 1956.

CRAFTS OF THE EARLY SETTLERS

Abrahamson, U., *God Bless our Home*. Toronto: Burns & MacEachern, 1966.

Guillet, E. C., *The Pioneer Farmer and Backwoodsman*. Toronto: University of Toronto Press, 1963. Vol. I and II.

Lord, P. S., Foley, D. J., *The Folk Arts and Crafts of New England*. Philadelphia: Chilton Books, 1965.

Minhinnick, J., *At Home in Upper Canada*. Toronto: Clarke Irwin, 1970.

Tunis, E., *Colonial Craftsmen*. New York: World Publishing, 1965.

MAGAZINES

The Beaver: Magazine of the North. Winnipeg: Hudson's Bay Company.

Canadian Antiques Collector: A Journal of Antiques and Fine Arts. Toronto: Canadian Antiques and Fine Arts Society.

Craft Dimensions Artisanales. Toronto: Canadian Guild of Crafts.

Craftsman: L'Artisan. Ottawa: Canadian Craftsmen's Association.

Index

Note: Italic numerals indicate drawings

187

Index of Craftsmen

*Note: * = works in Permanent Collection, Canadian Guild of Crafts / (Ontario)*

190

This volume was designed by Hugh Michaelson and
filmset in 12 point Palatino by Qualitype Company.
Colour separations are by Colourgraph Reproduction Inc.
Printed by Rolph-Clark-Stone Ltd. on
180M Georgian Offset smooth finish and
bound by John Deyell Company.